THE POLITICS OF
WRITING STUDIES

THE POLITICS OF WRITING STUDIES

Reinventing Our Universities from Below

ROBERT SAMUELS

UTAH STATE UNIVERSITY PRESS
Logan

© 2017 by the University Press of Colorado

Published by Utah State University Press
An imprint of University Press of Colorado
5589 Arapahoe Avenue, Suite 206C
Boulder, Colorado 80303

 The University Press of Colorado is a proud member of
The Association of American University Presses.

The University Press of Colorado is a cooperative publishing enterprise sup-
ported, in part, by Adams State University, Colorado State University, Fort
Lewis College, Metropolitan State University of Denver, Regis University,
University of Colorado, University of Northern Colorado, Utah State
University, and Western State Colorado University.

∞ The paper used in this publication meets the minimum requirements of the
American National Standard for Information Sciences—Permanence of Paper
for Printed Library Materials. ANSI Z39.48-1992

ISBN: 978-1-60732-583-3 (paperback)
ISBN: 978-1-60732-584-0 (ebook)

Library of Congress Cataloging-in-Publication Data

Names: Samuels, Robert, 1961– author.
Title: The politics of writing studies : reinventing our universities from below /
  Robert Samuels.
Description: Logan : Utah State University Press, [2017] | Includes biblio-
  graphical references and index.
Identifiers: LCCN 2016035664 | ISBN 9781607325833 (pbk.) | ISBN
  9781607325840 (ebook)
Subjects: LCSH: English language—Rhetoric—Study and teaching (Higher)—
  United States. | College teachers, Part-time—United States. | Universities and
  colleges—United States—Faculty.
Classification: LCC PE1405.U6 S255 2017 | DDC 808/.042071173—dc23
LC record available at https://lccn.loc.gov/2016035664

CONTENTS

THE POLITICS OF
WRITING STUDIES

INTRODUCTION

In *Reframing Writing Assessment*, Linda Adler-Kassner and Peggy O'Neill urge writing studies faculty to get involved in the conversations surrounding how writing, learning, teaching, and education are being defined: "Writing assessment, in other words, cannot be separated from these larger issues because these larger, contextual issues determine—whether directly or indirectly—much of what happens in postsecondary institutions and our programs and classrooms" (Adler-Kassner and O'Neill 2010, 4). Thus, composition instructors and researchers must think about how popular opinion and governmental policies are shaping not only education in general, but also, in particular, the teaching of writing. To be precise, the teaching of writing does not happen in a political and social vacuum.

As Adler-Kassner and O'Neill stress, the teaching of college composition is influenced by the different ways higher education is itself valued; for example, the ongoing debate of whether college is about training students for future jobs or democratic citizenship affects how writing is assessed: "As a subject that is considered central to students' successes when they enter college, during postsecondary education, and into careers, writing is often a centerpiece of discussions about (and, sometimes, a prescription for) what should happen in secondary and post-secondary classrooms in order for students to be prepared for the next steps" (7). This argument implies that writing studies cannot be removed from politics and public-policy debates, so it is necessary for teachers of college composition to seek to influence the ways writing and education are being represented. Ideology, then, cannot be removed from the classroom

DOI: 10.7330/9781607325840.c000

or research, and faculty have to involve themselves in the public framing of the value of higher education.[1]

Given the need for faculty to engage in this political process, it is disconcerting that some researchers in writing studies both express and repress the larger social and economic factors shaping college education today. Although many of the faculty discussed in this book do show a key awareness of the social forces affecting all aspects of student learning, there is a tendency to retreat into a hypothetical nonideological space in order to focus on the isolated student writer. In many cases, it appears that since people no longer believe there can be any real alternative to the current system, all they can do is critique the system as they try to conform to it. I argue that one of the dominant modes of subjectivity in contemporary culture and education is, in fact, cynical conformity, and this conformity entails people competing in a system in which they no longer believe.[2] We shall see that on all levels of education, students, faculty, and administrators are socialized to adapt to a problematic structure.

My central argument is that very little will change if we do not take on the larger issues that influence higher education. Writing studies may help improve some local situations, but this improvement will only create small exceptions that prove the rule, and the rule is that many forms of higher education instruction today are alienating, exploitive, and ineffective. To really change things, we must organize on a collective, national level to transform our institutions: we cannot simply try to function within the system and make our own programs more responsive to student learning. Ultimately, we must work together to get rid of the dependency on large lecture classes, standardized tests, student evaluations, college rankings, and just-in-time faculty.[3]

Instead of calling for the types of changes I discuss throughout this book, some writing studies theorists tend to seek intellectual solutions to structural problems. Thus, just as Marx critiques Hegel for only providing a spiritual fix to material conflicts, I argue that many of the current attempts to reform the teaching of college composition try to overcome material problems, like the exploitation of contingent faculty and graduate-student instructors, by positing theoretical and intellectual transformations. I also claim that the central institutional strategy found in many of the works I examine is based on the idea that if other disciplines and administrators just recognize that writing studies is also a discipline producing published empirical research, the field will be rewarded with more tenure-track positions and enhanced resources. In contrast to this strategy, I argue that the often-debased status of composition is not due to its inherent merits but can be attributed to its association with undergraduate education, teaching, students, practice, and form. Therefore, in the contemporary university, and in other institutions that conform to this system, prestige and power are maintained by reinforcing a set of hierarchies that place research over teaching and theory over practice.

Without organizing to overturn these oppositions, it is hard to imagine writing studies gaining more resources and institutional power. Moreover, if we aim to improve student learning by paying special attention to the ways students transfer knowledge from one context and genre to the next, then without changing the system, we may be just helping students conform to an alienating culture. In fact, the focus on assessment in writing studies can be read as an attempt to adapt to the growing accountability movement from a position of enlightened cynicism. Thus, as we depict the negative aspects of grading, testing, and ranking, we continue to perform these tasks from a position of self-reflective distance.

THE OUTLINE OF THE BOOK

This book traces the development of a new academic movement, which has been referred to as *writing studies*. As an offshoot of the field of rhetoric and composition, the central features of this new paradigm include a use of social science methodologies and a focus on the key concepts of transfer, genre, and metacognition. The argument here is not that other types of writing instruction and theory are no longer valid or apparent; rather, this book focuses on a specific group of researchers who are helping to build a new vision for the teaching of composition. Although my general approach is critical one, I also hope to show how this new movement can play an important role in transforming our universities from below.

The first chapter looks at two texts by Elizabeth Wardle, one singly authored by her and one coauthored with Doug Downs, in order to document the relation between the labor problems in composition and new pedagogical strategies in writing studies. Wardle is an interesting example because she does show a strong understanding of the ways the use and abuse of contingent faculty positions undermines composition programs, but at the same time, she tends to see curricular transformations as the key to overcoming these material issues. In proposing a writing-about-writing (WaW) approach to composition with Doug Downs, Wardle seeks to overcome the conflict between content and form by making composition research the content of composition courses. This self-reflexive gesture can be found in many aspects of contemporary society, and it often is based on the underlying idea that since there are no alternatives to our current system, all we can do is become more self-aware as we learn how to navigate exploitive material relations.[4]

In chapter 2, I turn to Anne Beaufort's longitudinal study of a single student writer in order to examine the way a focus on transfer and genre in writing studies has both positive and negative effects. On one level, these threshold concepts help us focus on the ways students actually write and learn in specific contexts, but this concentration on the individual student tends to drown out our need to change negative institutional structures.[5] Moreover, Beaufort's text reveals a troubling trend of writing studies specialists who call into question the possible effectiveness of college composition, especially the need for first-year writing courses.[6] By claiming students transfer very little from their composition classes to other classes and contexts, Beaufort and others may unintentionally feed into the defunding of writing programs and the humanities.

In chapter 3, I look at the book *Writing across Contexts* (Yancey, Robertson, and Taczak 2014) to see the ways in which the use of transfer, genre, and metacognition in writing studies can help us understand the contradictory nature of self-awareness in composition. The authors of this book do a good job of depicting the reasons K–12 education shapes college writers in a negative fashion, but their solution tends to be an emphasis on the individual writer who develops their own theory of writing. Once again, individual thinking is seen as the solution to material, political, and cultural problems.

Chapter 4 turns to Charles Bazerman's (2012) "Genre as Social Action." This important work examines the ways students must adjust the form and content of their writing to specific social contexts, so it appears to offer a more social and material understanding of composition; however, the underlying theories of communication and discourse presented by Bazerman tend to point to a conformist rhetoric. In short, students are urged to adjust their thinking and subjectivity to the mastery of particular social discourses, and underlying this social conformity is an understanding of communication that is at times problematic. Instead of stressing complexity, difference, dissensus, and overdetermination, Bazerman's theory returns to a pre-deconstructive understanding of writing.

Chapter 5 looks at Sid Dobrin's (2011) *Postcomposition* as another example of how writing studies theorists often try to overcome economic and political conflicts by retreating to a nonideological space. For Dobrin, this move entails a celebration of cyber posthumanism and the realm of pure theory. In an effort to escape the problems of administrative control, contingent faculty, required assessments, and educational defunding, Dobrin calls for a new conception of writing that eliminates the need for subjects, agency, planning, and activism; instead, he offers a network theory of recirculation that mimics many of the negative aspects of high-tech neoliberal capitalism.

In the final chapter of this book, I outline ways proponents of writing studies can work together to transform universities from the bottom up. By looking at such issues as faculty evaluations, class size, contingent labor, public funding, shared governance, and academic freedom, I outline a plan of action for transformative institutional change. All these interventions are necessary because we must realize that students' learning conditions are shaped by the faculty's working conditions, and these conditions are themselves influenced by larger economic and political factors.

NOTES

1. For more on defining the roles and values of contemporary higher education see David Kirp (2009), Robert Nisbet (1971), Bill Readings (1996), Robert Samuels (2013), and Jennifer Washburn (2008).

2. The theory of cynical conformity is discussed throughout Slavoj Žižek's (1989) *The Sublime Object of Ideology*.

3. Alfie Kohn's (2000) work on education does a good job of examining many of the problems concerning standardized tests, large lecture classes, and grading.

4. Mark Fisher's (2009) *Capitalist Realism* posits that a main aspect of neoliberal ideology is the notion that there can be no alternatives to the current capitalist system.

5. This book was informed by the notion of threshold concepts articulated by Linda Adler-Kassner, but it was written before Adler-Kassner and Wardle's (2015) book *Naming What We Know: Threshold Concepts of Writing* was published.

6. Other people in the field of composition who have called into the question the value of first-year writing courses are Sharon Crowley (1998), Sid Dobrin (2011), and David Smit (2004).

1
CONTINGENT LABOR, WRITING STUDIES, AND WRITING ABOUT WRITING

This chapter looks at two texts, one by Elizabeth Wardle and one by Wardle and Doug Downs, to examine the ways the use and abuse of contingent faculty in higher education affect the ability to implement a writing studies approach to the teaching of composition. Although I focus on research universities, many of the practices developed at these institutions are spreading to all forms of higher education in a globalizing mode of social conformity. On many levels, writing studies is itself structured by the contradictory nature of its relation to the dominant university research paradigm: while the teaching of writing challenges many of the standard institutional hierarchies, the desire for more resources pushes these composition programs to reproduce the structures that place writing, teaching, students, form, and practice in a debased position.[1] Wardle's work is important here because she both acknowledges the need for structural change and offers a curricular and theoretical solution.

My strategy in referring to Wardle's texts focuses on performing a close reading of her argument in order to both highlight her main contributions to the field and unveil what is still missing from her discourse. Since she is one of the most recognized scholars in the field of writing studies, her work is highly influential; however, it not my intention to argue that Wardle, or any other single contributor to the discipline, embodies the entirety of the discourse. Instead, I seek to look at the ways key texts are shaped by the political economy of neoliberal higher education. I also want to emphasize the importance of close reading and the need to avoid vague and distant summarizations. Since words and arguments matter, it is essential to look at how

DOI: 10.7330/9781607325840.c001

specific arguments are constructed by paying close attention to the unfolding of a particular text.

I also want to stress that I engage with her work through a series of ideological assumptions that concern the role higher education plays in the political economy of neoliberalism. Although many people define the current historical moment by the dominance of a conservative backlash against public institutions and progressive policies, I argue that it is also important to look at the ways liberals have actively participated in the reshaping of the political economy. For example, it is clear a conservative tax revolt has fueled an antigovernment movement, and this movement has resulted in the defunding of public universities and colleges. However, at the same time, liberal and progressive professors have helped construct and maintain a system that privileges research over teaching and individual rights over collective solidarity. Even though tenure was developed in order to protect academic freedom and shared governance, one must wonder why this system of job security has resulted in a structure in which the majority of the faculty do not have their academic freedom protected and are not able to participate in shared governance. The downsizing of the faculty and the rise of a business-oriented administration class in higher education, thus, must be tied to both internal and external forces.

In *Degradation of the Academic Dogma*, Robert Nisbet (1971) argues that research universities in America began to be restructured after World War II, when huge sums of government money were funneled into public institutions in order to support military and scientific research. According to Nisbet, research faculty quickly learned that prestige and high salaries could be attained by focusing on conducting funded research, and once these professors turned away from their teaching duties to focus on research, other people had to be found to instruct the students. From this perspective, the privileging of research over teaching and grant-funded professors over instructors was not the result of a decrease in public funding for higher education; instead, government support led to a change in the priorities and incentives of these universities.

Nisbet's narrative challenges several common understandings of the relation between higher education and neoliberalism; instead of placing all the blame on the decrease of public funds and the external political push to privatize public institutions, he shows how internal practices were influenced by an increase of public funding. Thus, before the current destructive defunding of public institutions, we already see a major restructuring of higher education, and the hierarchies developed then still tend to dominate today.

As I argue throughout this book, the privileging of research over teaching and science over the humanities has a major effect on the present and future of writing studies. Not only do these hierarchies help explain the shifting of teaching from tenured professors to contingent faculty, but we also find a debasement of undergraduate teaching and the promotion of theory and graduate education over more "practical" courses like composition and foreign languages. We shall see that Wardle is aware of all these institutional transformations, yet she tends to argue that the best way for writing studies to improve its status and funding is to conform to the dominant institutional structures.

LABOR AND WRITING STUDIES

Wardle (2013) begins her "Intractable Writing Program Problems, *Kairos*, and Writing about Writing" by highlighting the problematic relation between the theories of writing studies and the practice of actual composition courses.

> Macro-level knowledge and resolutions from the larger field of Writing Studies are frequently unable to inform the micro-level of individual composition classes, largely because of our field's infamous labor problems. In other words, composition curricula and programs often struggle to act out of the knowledge of the field—not because we don't know how to do so, but because we are often caught in a cycle of having to hire part-time instructors at the last minute for very little pay and asking those teachers (who often don't have degrees in Rhetoric and Composition) to begin teaching a course within a week or two.[2]

Here, Wardle correctly indicates that we cannot promote new pedagogical practices, theories, and research projects if we do not also deal with academic labor issues. As she stresses, it is hard to mentor and train faculty who are hired at the last minute and may not have expertise in writing studies. This important framing of the relation between research and teaching can help us to think about the political, economic, and institutional affordances shaping the possibilities of writing studies.

A concern for the material conditions structuring higher education weaves in and out of Wardle's article, and it is my contention that a close reading of her argument reveals a conflict concerning the ways positive change can be made at higher education institutions. On the one hand, Wardle points to large structural forces determining how writing is taught, and on the other hand, she seeks to provide a local example of how individuals at a particular location can enact new pedagogical models. The question remains whether a move to adopt a writing studies approach in the teaching of composition courses can be achieved without collective action dedicated to transforming our institutions of higher education. In other words, can new methods centered on research into genre, transfer, threshold concepts, and metacognition be applied if old institutional hierarchies are not confronted and transformed through organized collective action? If institutions value research over teaching, graduate education over undergraduate education, theory over practice, and content over form, can writing studies' focus on researching how undergraduate students learn and write take hold?[3]

For Wardle, material conditions and institutional expectations help define the possibilities and limitations of classroom practices: "Often these courses are far larger than the class size suggested by NCTE, likely because of the high cost of lowering class size and of widespread misconceptions about what writing is (a 'basic skill') and what writing classes do ('fix' writing problems)." From this perspective, the determination of class size is driven by an economic concern and an institutional interpretation: not only do institutions want to save money by having larger classes, but they rationalize this expansion by claiming

writing courses teach a basic skill and serve primarily a reme-
dial goal of fixing writing problems. In response to this analysis,
an important question to ask is whether economic concerns are
driving pedagogical expectations, or the reductive understanding of writing is producing a rationale for money saving. To be
precise, are economics producing cultural understandings, or is
culture determining the material conditions?[4]

THE RHETORIC OF POWER

As academic thinkers and people invested in the power of rhetoric, we often believe culture drives social institutions, so the
best way to change a system is to change the culture. However,
what if we have it backward and economic forces produce cultural interpretations? For instance, behind some of the recent
pushes to focus on a writing studies approach to the teaching
of composition is the implicit argument that the best way to
increase resources for these programs is to enhance the cultural
respect for the field. According to this logic, if writing studies
can be seen as a legitimate discipline with established research
methodologies, theories, and concepts, it will be treated with
the same institutional respect as other research-oriented disciplines. Yet, one must still ask whether this approach is too
focused on a rhetoric of logos and ethos. Furthermore, if the
major forces structuring the distribution of resources in higher
education are irrational and unethical, rational and ethical
appeals may not prevail.

It is my contention that the social hierarchies placing
research over teaching, the sciences over the humanities, theory over practice, and graduates over undergraduates are not
rational or ethical structures; rather, they are irrational power
structures rationalized after the fact in order to maintain a system of prestige and privilege. Moreover, these power structures
can only be countered by organized collective action, and they
will not be transformed by merely rational and ethical appeals.
This does not mean we should stop making rational and ethical arguments, but we must understand that these rhetorical

devices will not be enough. We should add to pathos, logic, and ethos a fourth category of social power.

INSTITUTIONS MATTER

In returning to Wardle's (2013) text, we see both the strength and weakness of her institutional analysis.

> In addition, composition courses continue to be housed largely in English departments, where they tend to get the least attention and funding of all the low-funded English programs and where sometimes faculty with little interest in or training to teach writing are nonetheless required to do so. Sometimes entire composition programs are staffed with brand new graduate students, many if not most of whom are graduate students in fields other than Rhetoric and Composition, and who have taken, at most, one graduate course in how to teach writing before walking into a classroom.

Wardle begins this important analysis by pointing out the problems many composition programs face because they are located in English departments, and they are often at the low end of the funding and prestige hierarchy.[5] Since theory and literature are privileged over practice and writing, the importance of writing studies is devalued, and the teaching of composition is seen as an activity that requires little expertise, experience, or concern. One of the main ways this dynamic has been countered is by the establishment of separate writing programs. In what is often considered a type of academic divorce, collective action changes the power relation by producing a new institutional structure. Here power and privilege are countered by a collective will to create a new system and set of material relations. Yet, rarely has this type of transformation been produced by compositionists convincing English literature professors to revalue writing and writing studies; instead, the divorce is made through institutional power structures and battles over scarce resources.[6]

In stressing culture over economics, Wardle argues that promoters of the field of writing studies must realize composition has been treated by management in a different way than other disciplines.

No administrator would ever send untrained faculty members or graduate students from another discipline to staff an entire segment of courses in, say, biology or history or mathematics or economics. Yet this happens every day in composition programs. Because of these and other entrenched practices, locations, and labor conditions, and despite our field's advances in how best to teach writing, we can still find composition classrooms where the students are learning modes or grammar or literature in formalistic ways, or are learning popular culture with little to no attention to writing itself, in courses sometimes if not frequently taught by faculty or graduate students with little to no training (or even interest) in teaching writing.

Once again Wardle hones in on the main problem, which is that teachers' working conditions shape students' learning conditions, but her analysis does not go far enough. Not only are first-year writing courses often devalued in the higher education institutional hierarchy, but many first-year courses are devalued and underfunded no matter the discipline.[7] The central problem then is not primarily an issue of the ways people see the teaching of writing; rather, the problem stems from the social hierarchies placing research over teaching, faculty over students, theory over practice, and disciplines over general education.[8]

CONFRONTING INSTITUTIONAL HIERARCHIES

Writing studies often flies in the face of the dominant social hierarchies shaping higher education because it uses research to focus on student learning and effective pedagogical practices. Moreover, the attention to which skills and knowledge transfer from one class to the next—and from inside and outside the academy—positions writing studies to be a major player in assessment and the evaluation of instructional quality.[9] Still, the problematic nature of labor conditions for writing instructors threatens to undermine the desire to produce specific outcomes: "The fact that research has suggested for many decades now that students in composition courses often do not reach desired course outcomes or improve as writers in measurable ways in one or two composition courses is not an unrelated problem. It seems reasonable to assume that if we staffed any set of courses in any discipline with teachers who had little training or interest in teaching them, we would likely see a problem in student achievement" (Wardle 2013). As several longitudinal studies have looked at what students learn and transfer into and from their writing courses, it has become apparent that students are often not learning and retaining the desired goals of courses.[10] Wardle argues that one reason for this failure to transfer is that the faculty teaching the courses have little training in writing studies. However, one unintended risk with this focus on transfer is that it can feed the current political ideology that blames teachers for all our educational and social problems. Without a focus on the larger economic and political forces shaping higher education practices, teachers become the solution and problem in every social issue.[11] In the case of higher education, the lack of expertise and experience of graduate-student instructors places them in a difficult situation: they are often pushed to teach courses outside their interests and knowledge, and then they are blamed for not being experts.

A materialist analysis of higher education tells us graduate students play a contradictory role since they are supposed to be students and teachers. For example, many graduate students are recruited for graduate programs in order to keep certain subdisciplines alive, but once they start to study, they are immediately asked to be teachers of courses outside their area of specialization.[12] One could even argue that the use and abuse of graduate-student workers has been a major driver in the casualization of the academic labor force. The fact that departments allow grad students to teach undergrad courses sends the message that one does not need a degree, or expertise, or even experience to teach at a research university. This system puts the bar of entry into the profession so low that the door is open for virtually anyone to teach required undergraduate courses. A reason, then, that there are so few jobs for graduate students after they earn their PhDs is that there are so many grad students and contingent faculty without degrees teaching the courses.[13]

As writing studies emerges as the dominant paradigm for the teaching of composition, this troubling use of grad student instructors becomes even more apparent. If writing is not just a practice but is also a subject of study, it requires expert practitioners with degrees and experience; however, the larger structures of higher education can undermine this quest for expertise. Wardle adds that this labor problem is enhanced by the fact that there appears to be little consensus in the field concerning what people are actually supposed to be doing:

> The fact that composition courses often do not seem to achieve desired outcomes is made more complex because our field does not necessarily agree on what appropriate outcomes are or should be for first-year composition. Despite the valiant and important efforts of those who worked (and continue to work) on the WPA Outcomes Statement, beliefs about what outcomes should be for composition still seem to vary widely. Should composition courses help prepare students for what they will write later? If so, what counts as "later"? School settings? Which school settings? Work settings? Personal settings? If transferable knowledge and skills are not the desired outcome, then what do we focus on instead? Self awareness? Cultural awareness? Artistic and creative enjoyment of writing?

One of the laudable aspects of writing studies is the fact that it continues to ask the question, what are the goals of writing courses and how can the attainment of these objectives be studied and monitored? Yet, even if a stronger consensus were reached in the field, the use of grad-student instructors and part-time faculty would make it hard to implement the accepted practices.

CONTINGENCY AND INSTRUCTION

Due to the temporary and transitory nature of academic labor in writing programs, administrators often fall back on prescribing simplistic and rigid syllabi: "Because labor is unstable, some programs attempt to ensure programmatic consistency by giving part-time teachers and graduate students (some of whom teach even their first semester as MA students) program syllabi and specific and fairly rigid assignments to teach." Although it may seem like a unified theory of writing studies would enable this type of programmatic control, the reality is that it takes a great deal of study and practice to become an effective teacher of writing. In fact, once we see writing studies as a separate discipline with its own key concepts, theories, practices, and body of research, a high level of professional development is required, yet the material conditions of these programs often prevent the needed focus on expertise and experience: "Many programs make efforts to provide ongoing professional development for adjunct instructors and graduate students, but these supports are in constant tension with material conditions related to pay and time constraints, including the fact that such underpaid adjunct instructors are often teaching numerous sections at multiple institutions, leaving them little time to participate in the life of any one department." It should be clear from Wardle's analysis that it will be hard for a writing studies agenda to be employed if current labor conditions continue. In short, we must promote a national agenda to promote full-time faculty with job security, fair wages, a career path, and professional-development funding in order to secure a place for writing studies.

While Wardle does not make a direct call for a national movement, she does realize why the current labor structure should be transformed: "Until all composition teachers have relevant theoretical and research-based knowledge about writing and teaching writing, and are treated as expert professionals by their institutions, any attempts at programmatic consistency seem bound to be reductionist. In other words, until composition faculty themselves have enough knowledge about writing research and theory to make their own informed choices about curricula, and to make informed arguments for changed material conditions, how can we move beyond a managerial mode in composition programs?" Thus, we need a national solution to the academic labor problem because as Wardle indicates, the only way to advance the field is to change the labor situation and the way people are trained and hired. Moreover, if only some institutions are able to hire expert full-time faculty, the myth that anyone can teach writing can continue to circulate.

By relying on a disposable labor force, any effort to enhance the status and consistency of writing studies is bound to fail.

> If teachers are passive recipients of curricula they didn't help shape and philosophies they don't share, it seems likely that they can only enact them in a formulaic fashion, if they enact them at all. Such formulaic teaching (which our legislative bodies seem intent on pushing us even further toward) simply reinscribes all of the problems I have been outlining above: composition teachers are not seen as professionals with specialized disciplinary knowledge, and stakeholders assume that anyone can teach composition; and, thus, anyone can be hired to do so at the last minute, since there must not be much to learn or prepare for in teaching a composition class. The teachers most willing to teach composition for $2,000/course and no benefits are often (but not always) least involved in the field's discussions about writing and writing pedagogy; in turn, the composition courses they teach may not be informed by the knowledge of the field, and students are then less likely to achieve desired course outcomes, all of which set composition courses and programs up to be viewed as anything but academic or scholarly. And the cycle continues.

Wardle here outlines the central dialectic between labor conditions and the field of writing studies: the more writing is seen as a simple skill that can be taught by anyone in a single lower-division course, the more the low pay for the teachers is justified, and the more an institution relies on insecure faculty, the more it must impose a reductive, rigid curriculum, which further devalues the labor of the instructors and the expertise of the discipline.

LOCAL VERSUS NATIONAL

Following this insightful analysis of the material conditions shaping writing studies, Wardle turns her attention to the ways an individual program can counter many of the problems discussed above, and here is where things get complicated. Although it is possible for individual programs to make improvements and enact the core principles of writing studies, it is unclear how such local actions deal with the national problems discussed above. After all, we have a national academic labor system, and as Wardle posits above, there are often shared understandings of writing pedagogy and writing faculty that transcend individual institutions.

The central focus of the rest of her article is on the development and the implementation of a writing-about-writing program, but I want to concentrate on her institutional arguments. For example, she argues that teaching about writing studies in a writing course cannot help but confront the academic labor problem: "If teachers must know the research of the field in order to teach composition classes, large groups of adjuncts can't be hired at the last minute and treated as expendable; rather, potential teachers must have some training (whether formal or informal) in rhetoric and composition." Wardle makes a clear rational claim for the need to hire expert teachers with the right degrees and experience, but it is unclear how this reasoned argument will counter the administrative desire to keep the cost of instruction low by hiring grad students and contingent faculty members to teach required undergraduate courses. At the heart of her claim is the idea that if the field can prove it increases student outcomes by professionalizing the discipline, administrators will naturally support hiring more expert faculty:

> When composition teachers have this sort of disciplinary knowledge, they can teach to informed outcomes without being forced to a prescriptive and reductionist consistency, and they can be engaged and rewarded as expert colleagues, rather than "labor" to be "managed." . . . This *should* result in better achievement of student outcomes related to writing. And better student outcomes with professionalized teachers *should* raise the status of composition courses and programs themselves.

This logical argument for enhancing the status of writing faculty by professionalizing the field and demonstrating student learning does not account for the fact that many established disciplines like math, biology, psychology, and sociology still rely on graduate students and contingent faculty to teach many of their undergraduate courses. Furthermore, one of the only ways professions like law and medicine have been able to control the wages and labor conditions of their members is by controlling credentialing. Laws, unions, and collective action—not logic and ethics—have served as the keys to maintaining labor standards.

If we look at other professions that have been able protect better wages and working conditions, we should insist that only people with PhDs in writing studies or closely related specializations should be allowed to teach composition at the college level, but this requirement has never been realized. In fact, instead of calling for the PhD in writing studies as the basic standard for hiring new faculty, Wardle opens the door to a compromised solution: "In sum, teaching declarative concepts about writing requires *knowing* declarative concepts about writing, which requires some familiarity with the research of Writing Studies. There are two ways to assemble a faculty with such familiarity: hire all Rhet/Comp specialists (an expensive and difficult proposition) or implement sustained, scaffolded support for composition teachers from all backgrounds so that they can gain familiarity with some composition research." Due to economic concerns, Wardle calls for a model of training people to teach in a writing studies mode, but this argument may not improve many of the labor and material problems she discusses throughout her article.

FROM THE NATIONAL TO THE LOCAL

In her analysis of her own program's implementation of a writing studies approach, we learn she relied on the good fortune of having certain institutional players who supported her mission:

> At UCF we encountered and were able to take advantage of a kairotic moment to use a writing-about-writing approach to address the set of problems I outlined earlier. Our experience demonstrates how a programmatic writing-about-writing approach with timed implementation and training improved professionalization, informed micro-level classrooms with macro-level disciplinary knowledge, and, through both of these, improved student

outcomes. For these changes to occur, particular institutional supports had to be in place, and an advocate in upper adminis-tration needed to serve as the catalyst to ensure the attempted changes came to fruition. Our experience at UCF demonstrates how deep cultural shifts and changed material conditions can be effected through a combination of kairos, piloting and assess-ment, advocacy, and laying bare our practices so that they are visible to stakeholders.

This stress on the chance event of having a group of support-ive administrators conflicts with the large structural issues she addresses throughout her work. After all, if we have a national labor and teaching problem, it is hard to see how this problem can be fixed by relying on the temporary support of local actors. In fact, Wardle describes some of her local good fortune:

> The Dean of Undergraduate Studies' role as an advocate for changes in the institutional structures around the writing pro-gram (as well as the math program, which is a story in itself) can-not be overestimated. Knowing that some new funding was going to be available through a tuition increase, she made a proposal to the President for reducing composition class size from twenty-seven to twenty-five and conducting a three-year study of smaller class size, providing comparison groups of nineteen. She also argued for six new full-time instructor positions, four in 2009–10 and two more in 2010–11. The President agreed to what she proposed, launching the President's Class Size Initiative (PCSI), with the understanding that everything we did would be audited, assessed, and presented to stakeholders at any time. Our Dean of Undergraduate Studies understood how funding worked, knew what funding might be available, and had access to one of the few stakeholders who could effect structural change immediately.

This was indeed a fortuitous set of circumstances and thus does not establish any type of model that can be followed other than hoping to get supportive administrators with extra funds and a desire to do something differently. If one of the main positive factors in developing this program was fund-ing to reduce the size of writing classes and hire more full-time faculty, it is hard to imagine how a similar program can be implemented without similar extraordinary resources. My argument does not undermine the value of Wardle's program, but it does question whether we can spread this type of teaching and learning if we are not getting the needed resources. In other words, writing studies cannot be implemented on a large scale if we do not change the labor and funding structures of higher education.

In her final rhetorical gesture, Wardle argues that change is possible, but that it must wait for the right moment:

> Our experience illustrates that sometimes there are moments when change is more possible than usual, and as rhetoricians and writing program administrators, we can and must be prepared to take advantage of them. We might fail, and the passing opening might close. But it is possible to leverage our field's knowledge and narrative to work with our good teaching faculty and make changes. Often our field's narratives about composition programs are about the forces at work that keep change from happening. But change is possible, and structures are created, destroyed, and recreated by human beings.

Wardle is right to stress the role we can all play in making social and institutional change happen, but her own story is reliant on a particular, local example of a fortuitous set of circumstances that would be hard to replicate across the country.

LABOR AND WRITING ABOUT WRITING

As Wardle's focus on labor issues attests, it is difficult to imagine how to utilize a writing studies' approach in a system that relies on untrained contingent faculty; however, as she argues in her article with Doug Downs, "Teaching about Writing, Righting Misconceptions: (Re)Envisioning 'First-Year Composition' as 'Introduction to Writing Studies,'" the way around this problem may be found in a new curricular model for composition. In examining Downs and Wardle's work, I argue that the current emphasis on transfer, genre, and metacognition in writing studies represents an important effort to make undergraduate-student learning the focus of research and teaching at American universities, but this projects tends to reinforce many of the academic hierarchies structuring higher education today.

TRANSFER VERSUS FYC

A common move in many writing studies texts is to use the concept of transfer in order to question traditional assumptions regarding first-year writing:[14]

> First-year composition (FYC) is usually asked to prepare students to write across the university; this request assumes the existence of a "universal educated discourse" (Russell, "Activity Theory") that can be transferred from one writing situation to another. Yet more than twenty years of research and theory have repeatedly demonstrated that such a unified academic discourse does not exist and have seriously questioned what students can and do transfer from one context to another. (Downs and Wardle 2007, 552)

As we saw above, part of this critique of the universal, first-year writing course is based on the notion that these courses tend to be taught by contingent faculty and graduate students with very limited training in the field, while the other part of this argument is that the current way of teaching students composition is ineffective because it is based on the false assumption that writing is a universal skill that can be taught in a single course. Moreover, the labor and the antiuniversalist arguments come together through the notion that what allows administrators to place unqualified people in the composition classroom is management's flawed understanding of what can and should be taught in an effective writing course. In fact, Downs and Wardle posit that some of the false conceptions regarding composition come from writing studies' own failure to examine the research and findings related to what students actually transfer from one context to the next:

> However, for all practical purposes, writing studies as a field has largely ignored the implications of this research and theory and continued to assure its publics (faculty, administrators, parents, industry) that FYC can do what nonspecialists have always assumed it can: teach, in one or two early courses, "college writing" as a set of basic, fundamental skills that will apply in other college courses and in business and public spheres after college. In making these unsupportable assurances to stakeholders, our field reinforces cultural misconceptions of writing instead of attempting to educate students and publics out of those misconceptions.

> When we continue to pursue the goal of teaching students "how to write in college" in one or two semesters—despite the fact that our own scholarship extensively calls this possibility into question—we silently support the misconceptions that writing is not a real subject, that writing courses do not require expert instructors, and that rhetoric and composition are not genuine research areas or legitimate intellectual pursuits. We are, thus, complicit in reinforcing outsiders' views of writing studies as a trivial, skill-teaching nondiscipline. (Downs and Wardle 2007, 552–53)

Here, the reductive understanding of composition is once again tied to the labor issue: since administrators and other people inside and outside academic institutions don't realize what teaching writing really entails, they do not think it is necessary to hire expert faculty. Furthermore, the common practice of teaching composition in just one or two first-year courses provides the illusion that writing teaches "skills" and not any content. In fact, it is the purported lack of content that feeds the notion of writing's being universal but empty.

The solution Downs and Wardle propose to many of these issues is to move from seeing composition courses as classes in how to write in college to classes about writing, which would entail a transition "from acting as if writing is a basic, universal skill to acting as if writing studies is a discipline with content knowledge to which students should be introduced, thereby changing their understandings about writing and thus changing the ways they write" (Downs and Wardle 2007, 553). The driving idea behind the writing-about-writing strategy is to make writing itself the disciplinary research content of writing courses. Thus, the divide between the empty universal form and the particular content is overcome by making the form the content. In what can be called a Hegelian reversal, the opposites of the dialectic are synthesized by overcoming their supposed differences on an abstract intellectual level.

THEORY AND PRACTICE

Downs and Wardle follow this equation of form and content with another dialectical synthesis:

> Despite the progress our field has made over the years at erasing theory/practice oppositions, it is still too easy to imagine pedagogy as "practice," removed from the realm of serious theory or research about the work or direction of writing studies as a discipline. Resisting the notion that talk about pedagogy is merely talk about "practice" is especially important to writing studies because our field is conceived—by those who fund it, those who experience it, and most of those who work in it—as primarily pedagogical. Part of our purpose here is to insist on the deep disciplinary implications of FYC pedagogy; a pedagogical move whose intention is to help resituate an entire field within the academy demonstrates that pedagogy has impact beyond the daily teaching to-do list. (Downs and Wardle 2007, 554)

By overcoming the standard conflict between research and teaching, writing about writing promises to increase the prestige of writing studies, but the question remains: how does one turn the practice of teaching composition into an established discipline?[15] The fundamental strategy revealed by Downs and Wardle is to find an intellectual way to overcome the academic hierarchies that place composition in a debased status. Therefore, instead of calling for an elimination of the structures placing research over teaching, content over form, and theory over practice, the idea is to dissolve these hierarchies on a theoretical and formal level. One of the assumptions here is that if other disciplines and administrators recognize the research-oriented disciplinary status of writing studies, universities will be more likely to respect and support this field and treat it like other established disciplines. Here, the strategy is not to intervene and try to change the material conditions through organized action; rather, the desire is to play by the rules and values of the already established hierarchy.

Just as Marx (1975) accused Hegel of taking an intellectual and not a material approach to social transformation, we see here how the dialectical process of combining opposites can create the illusion of overcoming structural hierarchies. Furthermore, instead of defending the importance of writing, form, and teaching, this strategy may function to reinforce the devaluing of these activities. For example, in an effort to copy the way other disciplines have received institutional support, Downs and Wardle call for the need to establish a major for writing studies: "The Intro to Writing Studies course would be akin to the introductory courses offered in all other disciplines (i.e., Intro to Chemistry or Intro to Philosophy) and would potentially serve as a cornerstone course for writing studies majors beginning to take root across the country. (Having a major, of course, dramatically changes a field's standing in the academy.)" (Downs and Wardle 2007, 554). By taking on the same values and practices of the dominant university research paradigm, it is hard to see how the labor condition of writing will change since the main reason administrators want to devalue composition courses is that so many students are required to take these courses, so in order to drive down the cost of undergraduate education, low wages must be justified. In other words, the cultural value of the field does not determine the labor value; instead, the desire to reduce the labor value is justified after the fact by a cultural argument. This structure is similar to the way discrimination often functions in capitalism: cultural hierarchies are employed to justify and rationalize the desire to drive down wages and extract surplus labor value. In turn, these hierarchies are used to maintain and police the already-established value system. Thus, it may be very hard to revalue writing courses and the field of composition since its devaluation already serves to rationalize a whole set of economic and cultural practices.

It is important to point out that this understanding of the relation between culture and economics is not only crucial to the desire to transform labor practices in composition programs, but it also shows we often exclude irrational economic exploitation from our rational understandings of how rhetoric and education function. Inherent in Downs and Wardle's argument is the idea that if other disciplines and administrators saw we are really just like them, they would stop forcing us to rely on exploited labor. From a rational (logos) and moral (ethos) and even emotional (pathos) perspective, this strategy makes sense, but it may not work in terms of the political economy of social hierarchies. Consequently, we must add to the trinity of rhetorical figures a fourth element, which we can call *dunamis* (Ancient Greek for power and the ability to cause change). Of course giving something a new name will not necessarily change practices, but we do need to think about how irrational power defies our ability to make standard rhetorical appeals.[16]

Instead of focusing on the power structures and vested interests that maintain composition in a devalued position, Downs and Wardle in this text seek to challenge the dominant idea that contentless writing courses teach universal skills:

> A number of assumptions inform the premise that academic writing is somehow universal: writing can be considered independent of content; writing consists primarily of syntactic and mechanical concerns; and academic writing skills can be taught in a one or two introductory general writing skills courses and transferred easily to other courses. The content-versus-form misconception—as old as FYC itself—appears in standardized testing, with the SAT "writing" test giving better scores to longer essays and completely discounting factual errors. It also finds its way into New York Times editorials, where no less a public intellectual than Stanley Fish argues that it is possible to, and therefore that FYC should, focus strictly on writing's grammatical forms and disavow interest in its content. (Downs and Wardle 2007, 554–55)

Downs and Wardle have set up the issue of how people conceive of composition courses as an opposition between an empty universal form and the full content of disciplinary research, but what if instead of combining the opposing elements, we worked collectively to reverse the hierarchies structuring higher education? In other words, what would happen if we organized to force institutions to value teaching, writing, practice, and form?[17]

Not only do Downs and Wardle want to question the traditional view of writing courses as universal structures dedicated to teaching form, but they also critique some of the broader visions of composition programs:

> The WPA Outcomes Statement adopted by the Council of Writing Program Administrators in April 2000 . . . highlights four major outcomes for writing instruction: rhetorical knowledge;

critical thinking, reading, and writing; processes; and knowl-edge of conventions. These outcomes, which reflect an ideology of access to the academy and a desire to prepare students for academic writing, are increasingly being adopted nationwide (Ericsson). But can FYC fulfill these expectations?" (Downs and Wardle 2007, 555)

Downs and Wardle argue that we cannot teach in a required first-year writing course the broad writing, reading, and think-ing skills often advertised by universities and colleges:

> While some general features of writing are shared across dis-ciplines (e.g., a view of research writing as disciplinary con-versation; writing strategies such as the "moves" made in most research introductions; specialized terminology and explicit citation—see Hyland or Swales, for example), these shared features are realized differently within different academic dis-ciplines, courses, and even assignments (Howard; Hull; Russell, "Looking"; Shamoon). As a result, "academic writing" is consti-tuted by and in the diversity of activities and genres that mediate a wide variety of activities within higher education; its use as an umbrella term is dangerously misleading. (Downs and Wardle 2007, 556)

Using the writing studies concepts of genre and transfer, the argument is that it is misleading to tell the public we can teach general skills when we know writing always occurs in particu-lar genres for specific contexts and each discourse community requires its own specialized terminology. The problems with this view are twofold: (1) it could promote the defunding of compo-sition classes and programs because they no longer claim to do what people want them to do; and (2) it dismisses the fact that we can teach some important generalizable thinking, reading, and writing strategies.

Like so many other theories of composition, the focus on what does not transfer in particular contexts and genres can function to further devalue the teaching of writing. In fact, there has been a long tradition of composition scholars calling for the end of first-year composition, but these theorists rarely take seriously the possibility that their efforts to delegitimize these required classes could result in administrators deciding there is no reason to fund writing courses and programs at all.[18] Furthermore, these calls often are attached to the idea that composition courses are currently failing to do what they say they are doing. Is it any wonder people do not want to support a field that regularly argues that the field is failing? Furthermore, this critique of first-year writing courses can serve to hide the problem of relying on just-in-time, insecure faculty. After all, if no one is teaching writing in an effective manner, why should anyone care if nonexperts are teaching the courses?

Instead of dismissing the value of these courses, we should reexamine the key role these required courses can play in helping students adjust to the types of writing, thinking, and reading that occur in higher education and beyond. For example, teaching students to always think about the purpose, audience, context, and form of each writing genre is a general approach that can be taught. Yes, students may not learn how to write like an expert for specific genres in a few weeks of study, but they can learn to detect formal requirements and apply general tools for critical analysis. Furthermore, if students do not have their particular grammatical and syntactical issues addressed in first-year writing courses, it is unlikely other faculty will ever take the time to work on these problems.

Another reason we should not dismiss the universal aspects of a writing course is that it is important to help students understand the modern universalistic approach to reason and mass education. At the heart of modernity, we find the quest for universality, objectivity, neutrality, empiricism, and skepticism.[19] These learning attitudes represent ideal forms of thinking that constitute the foundation of the modern university, and while universality can repress cultural specificity and individual uniqueness, it is still vital to get students to understand the foundations of modernity and the modern university. However, Downs and Wardle's stress on the specificity of particular discourses does at times appear to reject the very notion of modern universality and the possibility of teaching generalizable habits of mind: "Asking teachers to teach 'academic writing' begs the question: which academic writing—what content, what genre, for what activity, context, and audience? FYC teachers are thus forced to define academic discourse for themselves (usually unconsciously) before they can teach it" (Downs and Wardle 2007, 556). This conflict between the empty universality of academic discourse and the particularity of disciplinary genres may represent a false opposition, which is later overcome through intellectual mediation. While the emphasis on students' learning how to adjust to specific contexts can result in a discourse of social conformity, the devaluing of formal universality may undermine the collective nature of university discourse.

As Slavoj Žižek (1989, 80) has argued, the key to modernity is the establishment of an artificial mode of subjectivity, which in turn allows people to escape from their immediate immersion in tradition, nature, solitude, and unconsciousness. In modernity's break with the premodern, an artificial separation from the world is developed, and this new attitude allows for abstraction, generalization, logic, reason, and the scientific method. Of course, there are good and bad things about this social attitude, but the very meaning of the word *university* is derived from the *universal* application of reason. For example, when René Descartes declares all people have an equal ability to reason, we can argue that his claim is not true in reality, but the call for universality opens up a space for democracy and an ethics of universal equality. The democratic subject is therefore an artificial construct that works like the universal discourse of scientific reason, which might only be an ideal abstraction, but it still remains important for us to teach.[20]

SCIENCE AND CAPITALISM IN THE NEOLIBERAL RESEARCH UNIVERSITY

One reason it is so easy to devalue teaching in higher education is the notion that anyone can teach but only a few special people can do research. This neoliberal logic is in part derived from the way science has been combined with capitalism in the contemporary university. Due to the role of grants, intellectual property, and patents, scientific knowledge is now tied to an access to capital.[21] Many university leaders have argued that we know how to fund the sciences because they bring in extra funds, but teaching only costs money. Of course, this view discounts the money students bring in through tuition and state funding and the fact that many research grants fail to cover the full cost of projects, but this logic is still endemic to higher education.

Returning to Downs and Wardle, we find that the rejection of the universal writing course is coupled with a stress on particular expertise and a devaluation of the humanities: "These instructors are unlikely to be involved in, familiar with, or able to teach the specialized discourses used to mediate other activities within disciplinary systems across the university. In effect, the flavor of the purportedly universal academic discourse taught in FYC is typically humanities-based and more specifically English studies-based" (Downs and Wardle 2007, 556). The discourse of writing studies here not only devalues first-year writing courses but also feeds into the current devaluing of the humanities. After all, if the goal of a writing course is to teach students how to conform to specific expert disciplines, the humanities becomes just one discourse among the others. Furthermore, the humanities themselves suffer from the same universal tendencies dismissed by the focus on transfer and genre and the collusion between capitalism and the sciences.

In fact, one of the reasons the humanities have lost much of their funding is that writing programs have been breaking away from English departments. Once again, there are positive and negative aspects of this divorce, but what has not been fully considered is the way the turn to the social sciences in writing studies contributes to the loss of funding for the humanities and a move toward the dominant university research paradigm. Part of this stress on scientific empiricism can be found in the employment of the concept of transfer, which is often used to discredit the work of current and past teachers of writing:

> Our field does not know what genres and tasks will help students in the myriad writing situations they will later find themselves. We do not know how writing in the major develops. We do not know if writing essays on biology in an English course helps

students write lab reports in biology courses. We do not know which genres or rhetorical strategies truly are universal in the academy, nor how to help FYC students recognize such universality. According to David Smit's summary of what we know about transfer, assumptions of direct and automatic transfer from one writing situation to another are unfounded. With scant research-based information about how to best help students write successfully in other courses, FYC teachers do not know whether choosing genre A over genre B will be of service to students who must write genre B or genre C later on. In "academic discourse" FYC, then, instructors must hope that any writing instruction will help students in some way and/or limit their teaching to basic scribal and syntactic skills. (Downs and Wardle 2007, 556–57)

Although it is important to be self-critical, this summary of what transfer tells us about the teaching of composition could be used to completely defund and dismantle writing programs. After all, why support a field that admits that it does not know what it is doing and that it may be failing at some of its most important tasks?

It is possible that in order to clear a space for a new model of composition, the old and current models must be negated, but this theory of transfer is often employed in a highly overgeneralized way. In fact, David Smit's work mentioned in the passage above constantly repeats the same generalized message about the impossibility of generalizing. What Smit (2004) does not stop to consider is that his own writing strategy follows a classic humanities-based critical discourse. By arguing that specific discourse communities and writing genres are too particular to teach in a universalizing writing course, he falls back into a set of universalizing claims, which undermine from within his entire argument. Here we find what the French psychoanalyst Jacques Lacan (1998) called the split between the subject of the statement and the subject of the enunciation (26, 44, 138). Smit's central statement is that the teaching of writing most often fails because the teachers and the students are not experts in a particular discipline or discourse community, but his enunciation is a general claim not derived from any particular discourse or genre other than the universal academic discourse itself.

UNIFYING THEORY

As Downs and Wardle reveal, the focus on the contingent and the particular in writing and learning is at times combined in writing studies with a strong desire to offer a single, unifying theory to make sure everyone is teaching the same thing in the same way: "If writing studies as a discipline is to have any authority over its own courses, our cornerstone course must resist conventional but inaccurate models of writing. A reenvisioned FYC shifts the central goal from teaching 'academic writing' to teaching realistic and useful conceptions of writing—perhaps the most significant of which would be that writing is neither basic nor universal but content- and context-contingent and irreducibly complex" (Downs and Wardle 2007, 557–58). It does seem contradictory to argue in a universalizing and absolutist way that writing should be taught as being contingent and complex, but this contradiction helps reveal one of the main structures of neoliberal ideology, which is the ability to get people to believe they can embody contradictions without tension or conflict. For example, MOOCs are often sold as being both highly personal and massive, and like so many other aspects of new media globalization, the isolated individual is able to freely choose when to plug into an already constituted universal system. In the case of writing studies, we have seen how opposites are combined in a friction-free fashion: form becomes content, theory becomes practice, research becomes teaching, and the particular is universalized.[22]

Like Hegel's dialectic, the theory of transfer offers a universalizing discourse about the impossibility of universality, and one way this ideology is reproduced is by turning to a metadiscourse in which a splitting occurs between what one says (everything is contextual) and how one says it (everyone should know this universal truth). In the case of writing about writing, self-reflexivity opens up the space for a doubling discourse in which contradictory notions can be maintained without conflict, tension, or dispute.

THE SELF-REFLEXIVITY OF WRITING ABOUT WRITING

In their generalized description about what a writing-about-writing course would actually look like, Downs and Wardle point toward the value of having students study writing studies theory and research in a composition class:

> The course content explores reading and writing: How does writing work? How do people use writing? What are problems related to writing and reading and how can they be solved? Students read writing research, conduct reading and writing auto-ethnographies, identify writing-related problems that interest them, write reviews of the existing literature on their chosen problems, and conduct their own primary research, which they report both orally and in writing. This course would serve as a gateway to WAC and WID programs better able to address issues of specialized discourse within specific academic disciplines. (Downs and Wardle 2007, 558)

The move here is to avoid the faculty's lack of expertise in external discourses by turning inwards and asking students to study writing itself. This turn to metacogntive self-reflexivity brings up several questions: (1) Do students want to learn about writing studies research and theory? (2) Does self-reflective knowledge about writing help college writers write? (3) Does writing about writing represent an academic form of metafiction? (4) Does this focus on writing itself prevent people from learning at least something about other writing genres? and (5) Isn't this move the ultimate example of turning to a generalized academic theory about how academics think about theory and writing?

WAW AND METAFICTION

One interesting aspect of this move to a self-reflective discourse is that it mirrors the use of metafiction in many forms of contemporary media. There have been several different explanations of why we are witnessing so many movies about movies and songs sampling other songs, but some of the more intriguing theories are that,

1. self-reflexivity creates distance from characters and plot, which increases the role for the audience (Hutcheon 1988);

2. since we do not believe there are any alternatives to our current social and economic system, all we can do is become aware of our problems from a perspective of ironic distance (Fisher 2009);

3. since we have run out of new forms and content, a self-reflexive culture is centered on remixing, sampling, collage, and pastiche (Strinati 1993);

4. the author's knowingness of genre rewards and reflects the audience's knowingness (Hutcheon 1988);

5. in a media-saturated culture, media only reflects other media (Baudrillard 1993);

6. we conform with irony and distance to a system in which we no longer believe (Žižek 1989);

7. the hyper-self-consciousness of culture reflects the self-consciousness of people living in a state of new media surveillance (Fisher 2009).

These general cultural claims concerning metafiction and contemporary media may seem far removed from the idea of teaching writing about writing, but all these trends do share the same tendency to equate form with content and society with the self.

It should be clear here that in no way am I arguing Downs and Wardle intend to mimic the worst aspects of the culture industry and the surveillance state, but it is possible that the recent moves in writing studies are shaped by larger social and cultural forces. For example, when they lay out their general principles for a writing-about-writing class, the focus on reading stresses the key role metacognition plays in contemporary education:

> Though there are a number of ways to institute an Intro to Writing Studies course, our iterations of the course were designed according to shared core beliefs and a desire to resist and alter students' misconceptions about writing. The first of our shared beliefs corresponds with James Reither's assertion that writing cannot be taught independent of content. It follows that the more an instructor can say about a writing's content, the more she can say about the writing itself; this is another way of saying that writing instructors should be expert readers. When the course content is writing studies, writing instructors are

> concretely enabled to fill that expert reader role. This change
> directly contravenes the typical assumption that first-year writing
> can be about anything, that somehow the content is irrelevant
> to an instructor's ability to respond to the writing. (Downs and
> Wardle 2007, 558)

In another Hegelian twist, reading is combined with writing as
form is fused with content; meanwhile, a general method is pro-
posed as just one of a number of possible ways to teach writing.
The question then is, how is this combining of opposites made
possible through the turn to a self-reflexive activity? My theory
is that self-reflexivity allows the field of writing studies to imagine it can escape from the destructive hierarchies that shape
higher education today, which place the teaching of writing in
a debased state. Since we do not believe we can transform or
escape the current system, all we can do is find a way to conform to it from a critical distance, and this distance is generated
through self-reflexivity.[23]

For Downs and Wardle, a key aspect of this self-reflexive turn
is the idea that by requiring students to study research in writing studies, the students will become convinced that the field is
actually a discipline:

> In this course, students are taught that writing is conventional
> and context-specific rather than governed by universal rules—
> thus they learn that within each new disciplinary course they will
> need to pay close attention to what counts as appropriate for
> that discourse community. Taking the research community of
> writing studies as our example not only allows writing instructors
> to bring their own expertise to the course, but also heightens
> students' awareness that writing itself is a subject of scholarly
> inquiry. Students leave the course with increased awareness of
> writing studies as a discipline, as well as a new outlook on writing
> as a researchable activity rather than a mysterious talent. (Downs
> and Wardle 2007, 559–60)

In their desire for universities to recognize the value of the
field, these teachers try to get students to see writing studies as
a separate discipline. The logic appears to be that if students
buy into our discipline, surely others will do the same, but we
must remember that one of the key hierarchies in the university

is the one that places disciplines over students and teaching. After all, disciplines are built and maintained by policing the borders within a bureaucratic structure that rewards specialized research: students, teaching, and formal concerns may play a small role in the production of disciplinary prestige.

Instead of countering the dominant structures that privilege disciplinary expertise over novice students, Downs and Wardle try to imagine students as experts already:

> The course respects students by refusing to create double standards or different rules for student writers than for expert writers. For example, students learn to recognize the need for expert opinion and cite it where necessary, but they also learn to claim their own situational expertise and write from it as expert writers do. This respect for students is in accord with the field's ethos, thus blending a pedagogical advantage with a disciplinary one. In addition, creating high expectations for students aligns well with current learning theory: students can accomplish far more than we typically give them credit for being able to, if only we will ask them to do it. (Downs and Wardle 2007, 560)

Although the theory of transfer tells us writing courses often fail because the students cannot write or think like experts in the genres they are using, the idea here is that if we simply pretend students have expertise, they will see themselves as experts and act accordingly.

This treating of amateurs as experts returns us to the labor problem in writing studies. In the current educational system, the only way we can claim more tenure-track lines is if we pretend to be just like all the other respected research disciplines, but we can never win at this game because it is structured with us at the bottom. The move then toward self-reflexivity offers an imaginary solution to a real material problem. If we just imagine that all of the oppositions structuring our world can be combined in a seamless manner, we can enter a social space devoid of conflict, hierarchy, tension, or debasement. However, material hierarchies are not transformed through simple rhetoric, and thus instead of interpreting the world, we must organize to change it.

THEORY VERSUS PRACTICE

My critique of Downs and Wardle is ambivalent because once we get to their concrete proposals for the teaching of writing, we see that their suggestions are actually quite sound and effective. The problem then is that their theory of institutional change is in conflict with their actual pedagogical practices. To be more precise, they propose an institutional strategy that is highly problematic, but the actual courses they propose make a lot of sense. Theory here is in conflict with practice, and thus it is necessary to approach their contradictions with a contradictory interpretation.

Although I do not think we can change the institutional status of writing studies by conforming to the dominant university research paradigm, we can help students become better writers by following many of the ideas presented in Downs and Wardle's work. For instance, the description of the readings they use in their courses does show careful attention to the ways students actually think and write:

> The articles we assign vary, as do the ideas on which we focus; thus, we do not prescribe an "ideal" set of readings here. However, the common denominators among our readings are these: Material in readings is centered on issues with which students have first-hand experience—for example, problems students are prone to experience throughout the writing process, from conceptual questions of purpose, to procedural questions of drafting and revision, to issues surrounding critical reading; Data-driven, research-focused readings seem more useful than highly theoretical pieces. The former tend to be both more readable and more concrete, making them more accessible and relevant to students. (Downs and Wardle 2007, 560)

Here, the focus is on helping students understand their own writing and the composing strategies of other writers. This practice is highly generalizable and does appear to align with many of the ways people teach composition today. Of course, the major move is to replace theme-based readings with texts centered on writing itself.

Downs and Wardle also present a mode of pedagogy that places the teaching of writing at odds with the dominant structures of higher education: "To center the course on student writing and avoid merely banking information, students discuss, write about, and test every reading in light of their own experiences; they discuss why they are reading a piece and how it might influence their understanding of writing" (Downs and Wardle 2007, 561). By focusing on student participation in their own learning and a move away from the banking theory of education, they return to an emphasis on student learning and engaged participation, but we must realize these pedagogical practices are often at odds with the way many courses continue to be taught at research universities in the United States. Although Downs and Wardle remain silent on this institutional issue, they do provide a model of student-centered learning:

> Class time spent on readings focuses more on students' reactions to them than on the readings themselves; thus, our students write about issues raised by readings by responding to prompts such as, "How are your experiences with research writing like and unlike Shirlie's as Kantz describes them? What would you do differently if you could?" We find that students' responses initiate excellent class discussions, and that throughout the course students come back to ideas in the readings they write about to frame discussions about their writing experiences. (Downs and Wardle 2007, 561)

This emphasis on student thinking and writing is often in conflict with the dominant use of lecturing, large classes, multiple-choice exams, and grading in most university courses.[24] Students are therefore exposed to another model of learning, but the question remains, what happens when they enter their other courses?

The problem then is not so much that nonwriting classes utilize expert discourses students have not mastered; rather, research universities tend to undervalue engaged undergraduate education, and this neglect can leave students disengaged and alienated. In fact, a student once told me my class had made him realize his entire education had been ineffective, but he wondered what he could do if the rest of the university does not realize this ineffectiveness? One response to this student and all the other alienated students is that they must work with faculty and other stakeholders to transform the way all courses are being taught.

As Downs and Wardle indicate, another problem with education at research universities is that students often do little if any research: "The most noteworthy feature of the course is that students conduct primary research, however limited, on issues of interest to both themselves and the field of writing studies. Conducting primary research helps students shift their orientation to research from one of compiling facts to one of generating knowledge" (Downs and Wardle 2007, 562). This move to ask students to do their own research is an important way to break down some of the hierarchies pitting faculty against students and research against teaching, and yet, once again, we must wonder what happens when students are only exposed to this involvement in producing new knowledge when they are in isolated, devalued writing courses?

In many ways, the model of teaching Downs and Wardle present should be followed by all classes in all subjects at a research university because it challenges some of the artificial aspects of academic discourse:

> One conception of writing we strive to help students shift is imagining "writing" essentially as merely drafting a paper. The course design helps us show students that most scholarly researched writing in fact begins with becoming curious and establishing a question and moves through research. What students traditionally imagine as writing is actually only the final move in a much larger series of events. However, in our courses, students do arrive at this final move, presenting their research in both a significant written report and an oral presentation. (Downs and Wardle 2007, 563)

This method places students in a real situation of creating new knowledge and communicating that knowledge in an effective way. Instead of simply listening to an expert professor lecture about already-established knowledge, students are motivated to practice the essential aspects of academic research themselves.

The question remains whether writing studies can improve the status of its faculty and discipline while creating effective learning experiences for undergraduate students. Downs and Wardle help us solve the latter issue, but the former issue remains vexed. This conflict between effective teaching and ineffective institutional structures will remain until students and faculty organize to fight for a better system with better values and better practices.

NOTES

1. My conception of the dominant university research paradigm is derived from Marc Bousquet (2008), Kirp (2009), Nisbet (1971), Readings (1996), and Washburn (2008).

2. For more on the labor issues facing composition, see Bousquet, Scott, and Parascondola (2004) Robertson and Slevin (1987), Schell and Stock (2000), Tony Scott (2009), James Sledd (2001), and Donna Strickland (2011).

3. For more on the hierarchies shaping contemporary higher education, see Kirp (2009), Samuels (2013), and Washburn (2008).

4. Throughout the history of Marxism, there has been a debate concerning whether economics (the base) determines culture (the superstructure) or culture dictates economics. For a careful analysis of this debate see Kojin Karatani (2014).

5. See Bousquet (2008), Crowley (1998), Schell and Stock (2000), and Strickland (2011).

6. For a discussion of the separation of writing programs from English departments, see Strickland (2011).

7. This use of contingent faculty in courses from a wide range of disciplines is discussed in Eagan and Jaeger (2008).

8. My use of binary oppositions in my argument seeks to clarify the general trends in higher education; of course, there are always exceptions, but these exceptions help prove the rule.

9. See Adler-Kassner and O'Neill (2010).

10. Anne Beaufort's (2007) *College Writing and Beyond: A New Framework for University Writing Instruction* offers one of the first longitudinal studies of transfer from a writing studies perspective.

11. See Diane Ravitch (2013).

12. The contradictory nature of graduate-student instructors is discussed in Marc Bousquet's (2008) *How the University Works*.

13. See Bousquet (2008).

14. I discuss this use and abuse of the concept of transfer in chapter 2 of this book.

15. On the formations of disciplines, see Becher and Trowler (2001).

16. My concept of power is in part derived from Jacques Derrida's (1978) reference to force in *Writing and Difference*.

17. Downs and Wardle's (2007) work also may appear to support a tendency in writing studies to dismiss the importance of teaching students how

to improve their grammar and syntax in a college writing class. One of the reasons for this downgrading of the need to teach mechanics is the fact that people often do not think of grammar as an essential rhetorical device. Although in the current structure, teaching, writing, practice, and form are devalued, these values must be countered, not reinforced.

18. See Crowley (1998).
19. See Descartes (1996).
20. For a detailed examination of the role of universality in universities and modern reason, see Colm Kelly (2012).
21. See Washburn (2008).
22. One of the key Hegelian aspects of these combinations is the use of rhetorical tricks to overcome material oppositions. For example, Hegel used the fact that in the German language, the word *Geist* means both mind and spirit in order to maintain a premodern religious discourse and modern scientific discourse at the same time.
23. For an insightful analysis of the relation between irony, metafiction, and contemporary society, see R. Jay Magill (2009).
24. See Samuels (2013, 27–37).

2

THE POLITICS OF TRANSFER
Grades, Meritocracy, and Genre in Anne Beaufort's College Writing and Beyond: A New Framework for University Writing

In the previous chapter, I outlined the institutional strategy of many proponents of writing studies, which is to gain prestige and funding for composition programs by replicating the dominant university research model. Part of this process involves establishing key concepts like genre, transfer, and writing about writing and developing a respected body of research. As we shall see in this chapter, this desire for disciplinary respect and needed resources often pushes the field to replace a humanities-based discourse with one derived mostly from the social sciences. Thus, instead of engaging in collective action to transform the destructive hierarchies shaping universities today, the new emphasis is to conform to current structures in order to compete for scarce resources. However, as I argue in the previous chapter, the problem with this strategy is that it fails to confront the fact that writing, undergraduate education, practice, and teaching are often debased in a system that privileges research, graduate education, and theory. Therefore, the effort by writing studies specialists to join the club of prestigious research disciplines may only function to reinforce the political and economic hierarchies that devalue the teaching of writing to undergraduate students.

As an example of the turn to a social science research model for writing studies, Anne Beaufort's (2007) *College Writing and Beyond: A New framework for University Writing Instruction* offers one of the most detailed longitudinal studies of the ways an individual student uses knowledge learned in their college writing courses to approach other courses and work after college.

DOI: 10.7330/9781607325840.c002

Because Beaufort's study resulted in a key text in the literature of transfer, it is important to look at the political assumptions and implications of her approach and analysis. Although many other people have examined her methodology, the approach here is to focus on the acknowledged and unacknowledged role played by institutional forces in the writing classes she examines.[1]

At the start of her book, she clearly places the issue of what students learn and transfer in a writing course into a larger social framework: "Freshman writing, if taught with an eye toward transfer of learning and with an explicit acknowledgement of the context of freshman writing itself as a social practice, can set students on a course of life-long learning so that they know how to learn to become better and better writers in a variety of social contexts" (Beaufort 2007, 7). As Beaufort correctly emphasizes, even though writing is often done by an individual writer for individual purposes, writing is still a social activity shaped by specific social contexts. In terms of writing studies, the focus on what knowledge transfers from one experience to the next is tied to the idea that writing is always shaped by particular genres, and these genres in turn are shaped by social contexts and institutional structures. However, the problem remains concerning the ways teachers and theorists of writing can incorporate a broad understanding of social contexts into their practices and theories.

ABOUT DISCIPLINE

As a way of thinking about the multiple social factors facing writing instruction and writing studies, Beaufort outlines an expanding circle of cultural and institutional factors. For instance, in response to critics who question the value of first-year writing classes, she offers the following multifaceted analysis:

> The first critique they make is based on social constructionism and activity theory and the related perspectives of literacy studies, genre theory, and critical theory. From these theoretical vantage points, all acts of writing—and writing instruction—are viewed as socially situated human activities. Writing literacy is

a form of political and social capital. Genres perform social functions. Writers assume subject positions and political positions through the genres they employ. This leads to a critique of freshman writing that goes something like this: because it is a compulsory course, taught in isolation from other disciplinary studies at the university as a basic skills course, this social context leads freshman writing to become a course in "writing to produce writing" (Dias 2000), or to "do school" (Russell 1995). For the majority of students, freshman writing is not a precursor to a writing major. It is an isolated course, an end in itself, a general education requirement to be gotten out of the way. If taught within an English department, or by teachers who are primarily trained in English or comparative literature, students may perceive it as an English course, and yet the course is often a poor step-child to literature courses in English or comparative literature departments and usually suffers the same isolationist lack of intellectual and social moorings. (Beaufort 2007, 9–10)

Since the writing studies theory of genre stresses the fact that all writing is shaped by particular social contexts, it becomes necessary to place the teaching of writing itself within a larger social analysis; however, the problem Beaufort confronts is what to do about composition's marginal status within higher education institutions. While writing is often taught in an isolated course as an isolated activity, required writing courses can be seen as classes centered on training students to conform to the generalized expectations of college discourse.

Beaufort posits that composition opens itself up to this reductive understanding of college writing courses because it is not tied to a specific body of research and disciplinary prestige:[2]

But why does this lack of institutional grounding for freshman writing matter? Because usually there is no overt linking of the course to any intellectual discipline (even the disciplines of Rhetoric or Composition Studies are usually not invoked in freshman writing), the over-riding social context for students becomes the institutional requirement of the course itself. So writing papers is perceived by students as an activity to earn a grade rather than to communicate to an audience of readers in a given discourse community and papers are commodified into grades, grades into grade reports, grade reports into transcripts, etc. This condition is a serious detriment to motivating

> writers and to teaching writers to be sensitive to authentic social
> contexts for writing. This condition also misleads students into
> thinking writing is a generic skill that, once learned, becomes a
> "one size fits all" intellectual garb. (Beaufort 2007, 10)

Although Beaufort wants to argue that the separation of composition from disciplinary knowledge undermines its institutional power and prestige, her analysis is really about the way all
courses in higher education have been affected by a social discourse of meritocracy and competitive individualism. The problem, then, is not that composition has been reduced to a service
course wherein which student work is commodified into grades;
rather, the problem is that all of education has been subjected
to a regime of replacing process with product and learning with
earning (grades, credits, degrees, merit).[3]

Since composition instructors must work closely with students,
and writing studies often examines what students do and do not
transfer from one context to the next, teachers of writing cannot
help but confront some of the negative forces shaping higher
education in general. In many ways, composition is a symptom of
the neoliberal university and thus represents the repressed anxi-
ety affecting all disciplines. A problem therefore with Beaufort's
analysis is that her focus on individual writing courses and a particular individual student prevents her from fully dealing with
the larger implications of her findings. Therefore, even when
she highlights larger structural issues, she quickly returns to the
question of what individual students learn in individual writing
courses taught by individual writing instructors.

This focus on the individual is combined with a theory centered on the idea that writing always occurs in a specific context
and genre, and this specificity means there are no general skills
or knowledge to be taught:

> Most teachers of writing think of themselves as generalists. The
> particular institutional context of their classes and the future
> endeavors of their students are of less concern than the chal-
> lenges of equipping students with basic skills. But research in
> composition studies and linguistic anthropology and literacy
> studies in the last 30 years has shown there is really no viable

> commodity called "general writing skills" once one gets beyond
> the level of vocabulary, spelling, grammar and sentence syntax
> (and some would argue that even at the sentence level, writ-
> ing is specific to particular discourse communities' needs).
> (Beaufort 2007, 6)

Beaufort here stresses a commonplace associated with the writing studies stress on genre and transfer, which is that there are
no general writing skills and every act of writing is defined by a
particular situation and context.[4]

GENRE, TRANSFER, AND THE ISOLATED STUDENT

When we combine Beaufort's focus on individuals with her theory of genre and transfer, we find the writing studies tendency
to emphasize how isolated subjects conform to specific social
situations. Therefore, since general writing skills are displaced
by particular discourse communities, there is a constant return
to the ways isolated individuals assimilate specific social contexts
within an educational system that rewards competing students
for their individual efforts. Moreover, this stress on isolated students is combined with a focus on particular teachers and the
failure of students and teachers to transfer learning from one
educational context to the next:

> McCarthy's landmark study documented how little a student
> may gain from a generic writing skills course. Others have
> repeatedly documented over and over the context-specific
> expectations about what counts as "good writing" (Bazerman
> 1982; Berkenkotter et al. 1988, Brandt 1990; Canagarajah 1997;
> Fahnestock and Secor 1991; Faigley and Hansen 1985, Heath
> 1983). Writing standards are largely cultural and socially spe-
> cific. And yet, novice writers usually get little instruction in how
> to study and acquire the writing practices of different discourse
> communities. (Beaufort 2007, 7)

One of the problems with this analysis is that it follows the now-
standard public discourse of blaming teachers and students for
educational failure instead of looking at larger social and institutional factors. Thus, even when Beaufort points out that what
qualifies as good writing is shaped by history and a whole host of

other social factors, she focuses on how individual instructors fail to teach individual students how to write for particular contexts:

> Given the way freshman writing is typically taught, graduates of these courses could easily think the standards for writing they have been given in freshman writing are universal. They are ill prepared to examine, question, or understand the literacy standards of discourse communities they are encountering in other disciplines, in the work world, or in other social spheres they participate in. This can result in negative transfer of learning: what worked for a freshman writing essay is inappropriately applied to writing in history, or social sciences, or the sciences or in business. The student must learn, through failed attempts at such transfer of supposed "general" writing skills, how to adapt to the standards and purposes for writing in new discourse communities. And there is significant documentation of students' inabilities, unassisted, to grasp these discourse community differences that affect writers' roles and the texts produced. (Beaufort 2007, 7)

While it is important to stress the role played by particular social contexts and specific discourse communities, this critique of general writing skills may not only serve to justify defunding first-year writing courses, but it can also function to devalue certain near-universal aspects of learning, thinking, and writing.[5]

As we teach students how to write for specific situations, it is still necessary to teach general principles of grammar, organization, logic, coherence, and academic discourse. Eliminating the notion of general writing skills makes it hard to counter the neoliberal stress on the isolated individual adapting to specific social reward systems. Furthermore, if we do not teach grammar as a mode of organization and communication, we undermine our ability to help our students become more effective writers, as we give them no alternative but to conform to particular discourses, communities, and genres.

Since grading rewards individual students for their ability to conform to particular educational expectations, it is hard to imagine how individual teachers can change the learning attitudes of their students. Beaufort, at times, is aware of this problem:

> While a more overt disciplinary basis to the writing instruction can solve the problem of writing that is devoid of a well-identified

> social context within which the writing is grounded and moti-
> vated, research in these approaches to writing instruction has
> uncovered other problems. Dias points out: "Writing [can be]
> defined . . . in the disciplinary courses primarily as a way of
> displaying learning." So teachers give assignments that lead
> students to feel they are simply demonstrating that they read
> the book or listened to the lectures rather than their engaging
> in the intellectual work of the discipline through writing tasks.
> (Beaufort 2007, 10)

Since students have been trained from an early age to write
in school in order to be tested on what they have learned, the
writing studies focus on intellectual work is challenging, and
this focus is another reason writing courses often come into
conflict with the dominant mode of teaching and learning in
higher education.[6] As Beaufort points out, "The student knows,
and the teacher knows, the writing is for purposes of gate-keep-
ing/grade-giving" (11). Once again, it is hard to imagine how
a writing studies' pedagogy can be implemented in an educational structure that has prioritized meritocratic social sorting
over learning.

THE PARTICULAR UNIVERSAL

Another way composition courses counter dominant trends in
higher education is by seeing writing as a specific activity and
not as a transparent medium: "Russell (1995) says, 'A discipline
uses writing as a tool for pursuing some object. Writing is not
the object of its activity. Thus, writing tends to become transparent, automatic, and beneath the level of conscious activity
for those who are thoroughly socialized into it. . . . As a result,
experts may have great difficulty explaining these operations'"
(Beaufort 2007, 11). Once again, the larger institutional and
cultural context of education tells us that in order for writing
to be seen as both an activity and a subject of study, it must confront the dominant model of learning that emphasizes grades,
content knowledge, transparent language, and theory over practice. Writing studies is thus a pedagogical countermovement

that requires a plan for how to change the priorities and practices of higher education.

Even though Beaufort does not make the argument for larger structural changes, she posits that one way of making writing instruction more effective is to focus on how experts in particular disciplines and discourse communities rely on a specific knowledge base:

> Besides the knowledge entailed in understanding and engaging the broader goals and activities of a discourse community, writers must engage a specific subject matter considered within the purview of a discourse community. In this aspect of writing, experts are both drawing on existing knowledge bases (i.e. background knowledge) and doing the critical thinking necessary for the creation of "new" or "transformed" knowledge (Bereiter and Scardamlia 1987; Bloom 1971) that is interactive with and is influenced by the discourse community. Such critical thinking includes knowing how to frame the inquiry, what kinds of questions to ask or analytical frameworks to use in order to "transform" or inscribe documents with new meaning. (Beaufort 2007, 15)

The paradox of this analysis is that on the one hand, it stresses the role played by specific knowledge for specific disciplines, and on the other hand, it highlights general thinking strategies, which can be taught in a universal writing course. In fact, I argue that some proponents of writing studies emphasizing genre and transfer tend to undervalue the key role the teaching of general habits of mind can play in a first-year writing course. After all, if we want students to be able to detect the typical features of specific writing genres, we must teach them how to analyze discourses and frame inquiries by following generalizable thinking strategies.[7] In other words, students can learn in a first-year writing course to look for voice, audience, format, and other formal elements by applying general principles of academic discourse.

At the same moment Beaufort states that the specific requirements of particular genres counter the more universal aspects of first-year writing courses, she applies near-universal categories in her theory:

> In addition to discourse community knowledge, subject matter knowledge, and genre knowledge, writers must address the specific, immediate rhetorical situation of individual communicative acts (Ede and Lunsford 1984, Lunsford and Ede 1996). This includes considering the specific audience and purpose for a particular text and how best to communicate rhetorically in that instance. The rhetorical moment is also affected by the social context—material conditions, timing, social relationships, etc. within the discourse community. And finally, writers must have writing process knowledge, i.e. knowledge of the ways in which one proceeds through the writing task in its various phases. This procedural knowledge associated with writing process is also affected by the material, socially specific particulars of a given writing situation or "community of practice." (Beaufort 2007, 16)

I argue that this passage is structured by the universal dialectic between general rhetorical features and specific discourse communities and that the metaknowledge structuring her analysis is itself highly generalizable. To be concise, the theory that all writing occurs in discrete discourses is itself a generalized claim presented within a self-reflexive, universalizing discourse.

My point in underlining the role played by general claims in the focus on specific discourses is not to simply locate a potential contradiction in Beaufort's work; rather, my goal is to show that one of the most important things we can teach students is the underlying habits of mind that must be taught in order for students to be able to detect the typical features of specific genres. This argument must be made in order to defend the importance of required first-year writing courses and to provide a more realistic notion of how people actually learn. In the case of writing studies, the undervaluing of general thinking and rhetorical strategies can result in the problematic claim that only experts in particular disciplines can teach writing because all writing is highly specific and genre based. At times, Beaufort does make this discipline-centered claim: "Gaining writing expertise only takes place, I believe, in the context of situational problem-solving, or, as others have demonstrated, through legitimate participants in apprenticeship situations (Heath 1982; Lave and Wenger 1991; Prior 1994)" (Beaufort 2007, 18). This hypercontextualist perspective devalues the more general writing and thinking strategies that can be taught in first-year writing courses.[8]

COLOR-BLIND MERITOCRACY

It is interesting to note that at the same time Beaufort privileges specific genres and discourse communities over general rhetorical modes of analysis, she returns to a modern universalistic approach to the question of the political implications of writing studies: "To those who do not feel satisfied that there is enough of a critical, liberal agenda in this theory of writing expertise, I would say, yes, the theory is apolitical in the sense that no particular political agenda is being promoted and no one interest group is being catered to. But on the other hand, this view of expertise is crucial to the legitimate social causes of literacy, employment, and effective communication—to empowering all across gender, race, ethnic, and class lines to write effectively in a range of social contexts"(Beaufort 2007, 18).[9] This gesture of highlighting the empowerment of student writers regardless of gender, race, ethnic, and class differences echoes the conservative attempt to use the liberal notion of equality in order to deny the ways prejudice and inequalities still shape contemporary society.[10] As many academic thinkers have pointed out, the claim to be apolitical or nonideological is an ideological and political move. What is so strange is that a writer who emphasizes the crucial role played by specific social discourses would turn around and make a claim for a color-blind universalistic discourse. One possible explanation for this separation of expertise and demographic differences is that within the logic of meritocracy, everyone is supposed to be judged for their individual talents and knowledge and not on broader social categories. The central problems with this theory are that there is no perfectly fair and equal system of judgment and every meritocracy soon becomes an aristocracy because the people who succeed rewrite the rules to maintain power.[11]

Since a meritocracy stresses the equality of opportunity and not the equality of outcomes, the winners of the meritocratic competition can claim that social inequality does not matter because everyone has the same chance of succeeding. In terms of writing studies, this meritocratic logic seeps into the stress on transfer and genre because individual students are judged based on their ability to successfully adapt to new expert situations. In fact, like many other theorists of genre and transfer, Beaufort employs a generalized model of intellectual development to support her notion of how people learn and write in specific contexts:

> Bloom's (1971) hierarchy of critical thinking skills, which was an extension of Piaget's schema of concrete versus formal operations and has been employed extensively in writing curriculum development, is a useful tool for analyzing writers' critical thinking skills and for developing assignment sequences, even though its ability to distinguish the fine points of critical thinking skills is limited. Even within different types of cognitive work (summary, seriation, classification, analysis, etc.) there can be gradations from simpler to more complex tasks (Kiniry and Strenski 1985), so what constitutes a "hierarchy" or progression from easier to more complex cognitive tasks is not so easily mapped out and more than one cognitive process may be employed in composing a single text. The domain-specific nature of critical thinking must also be taken into consideration. (Beaufort 2007, 21)

Beaufort may not fully endorse this developmental model because of her stress on domain-specific knowledge, but her discourse does constantly return to the idea of assessing an individual student's ability to transfer knowledge from one situation to the next, so she does combine a meritocratic logic of assessment with a meritocratic notion of recognized expertise: "Yet in spite of various schematics of distinct types of critical thinking, generally there is agreement that indicators of more fully developed thinking skills as applicable to academic writing tasks include the ability to manipulate source texts in complex ways beyond simple restatement or recall, the ability to entertain more than one point of view, i.e. to do relativistic thinking on complex issues, and the ability to think metacognitively about one's own thinking" (22). These generalizable mental processes are placed within a discourse that tends to downplay the importance of teaching generalized knowledge, and this paradox can be in part explained by the need to hold on to a value-free notion of meritocratic expertise.

Within the discourse of what students do and do not transfer from one course to the next, the use of expertise often functions to produce a social hierarchy of learning. For example, in Beaufort's use of Patricia Alexander's model of development, we find a stratified meritocratic logic: "Rather than sharp distinctions between 'novice' and 'expert,' she conceptualizes a continuum in three phases: (1) acclimation (the learner has limited and fragmented knowledge; (2) competence (exhibiting domain knowledge that is cohesive and 'principled in structure'; and (3) proficiency (a broad and deep knowledge base and the ability to build new knowledge in the domain)"(Beaufort 2007, 25). As with all developmental models, the problem with this theory is that it easily falls into a reductive system for social sorting: at the bottom level we have the novices; next, we have the competent; and eventually, we have the experts. For an "apolitical" system, it is hard not to notice how this developmental model of transfer reinstates a traditional class-based political hierarchy.

CLASS IN THE CLASS

Beaufort's desire to focus on a nonpolitical notion of writing expertise and writing instruction is threatened by her own acute awareness of how composition is always affected by politics, labor, and institutional hierarchies. For instance, she begins one chapter by highlighting different conversations regarding who teaches writing and what institutional factors shape how faculty think of composition. In her first example, a department chair deals with the conflict between teaching and research:

> "It's very hard to get people to volunteer to teach Freshman Writing. It used to be routine, but there was a major change in the 1960s and 1970s. Since the 1970s research has been valued more. . . . Over the years there's been involvement of the faculty in Freshman Writing. We want to reestablish it. . . . The

> deans have demanded it. It's not the best use of faculty time and course distributions and they won't do as well as the lecturers because they've been out of the field. But here power flows from above. The penalty is no bucks. But on the positive side, some faculty involvement will show how good the program is." After the tape recorder is turned off, the chair points to several textbooks authored by freshman writing lecturers on his desk and says, "These don't carry any status. They're not the books that get written up in *The New York Times Book Review*." (Beaufort 2007, 28–29)

This passage focuses on many of the different ways writing and teachers of writing are devalued at research universities. The first conflict is that teaching writing is seen as a distraction from the more important task of doing research, and even when writing instructors do produce books in composition, their research is not respected because it does not get reviewed by the *New York Times*. The other way the irrational hierarchies structuring higher education institutions are exposed here is by the dean's positing that research professors will probably not be good writing instructors because they have been out of the field, but by simply placing these professors in the composition classroom, the department signals that it values the teaching of writing. The flip side of this logic is that when composition programs employ contingent faculty and graduate students to teach their composition courses, they devalue the courses since prestige is derived from faculty status and not faculty expertise. In this case, the meritocracy has reverted to an aristocracy or some weird combination of the two views.

In Beaufort's next sampling of the vexed role of labor in writing instruction, she turns to the administrative view of composition:

> The freshman writing courses serve two educational functions. First . . . is to improve the skills of freshmen in writing, argumentation, and library research. The second is to give graduate students in English an opportunity to develop skills in teaching an undergraduate composition course. (A third function is to provide financial support for graduate students in English). (Beaufort 2007, 29)

This parenthetical reference to using composition courses in order to help support graduate students in English points to one of the main problems with the system: since many administrators think anyone can teach writing, these courses can be used to employ virtually anyone. The end result of this logic is that writing and writing faculty are devalued because graduate students are used as cheap labor; meanwhile, the research prestige and expertise of the field of writing are downsized.[12]

Many writing studies enthusiasts believe the best way to overcome this devaluing of composition and writing instructors is to convince administrators and other faculty that writing has its own research and disciplinary expertise and therefore writing studies should be rewarded with respect and tenure-track lines; however, the passages cited above reveal that institutions have a great monetary incentive to devalue writing instruction and the field of writing. Since so many students are required to take writing classes, it makes administrative sense to find the cheapest way to run these courses, and this means part-time faculty and graduate students must teach these courses. Furthermore, in order to provide financial support to graduate students from different departments, it becomes necessary to argue that anyone can teach writing courses. In response to this economic logic, a writing studies proponent may argue that if everyone becomes convinced writing is a research discipline with specific expertise, only credentialed experts in writing studies should teach composition courses. Yet, the fact that writing programs themselves regularly hire graduate students and part-time faculty to teach their courses undermines the ability to make this claim concerning expertise.

As Beaufort points out, even though the required writing course is ignored by the tenure-track faculty, what cannot be ignored is that while the freshman English budget was $800,000, the revenues from freshman English tuition were estimated to be $2.5 million. One way of reading this financial arrangement is to realize writing instruction must be devalued in order to justify the low pay of the people teaching the courses so the writing program can generate a profit to support the faculty and administrators who devalue writing. However, instead of challenging this unjust financial arrangement, Beaufort cites a senior English department faculty member who rationalizes simply scrapping the first-year writing requirement: "This year's discussions of possible effects of budget constraints on the Freshman English Program come at a time when many colleges and universities committed to excellent teaching are rethinking the substance and direction of their programs. . . . Most relevant research findings for current changes has been the overwhelming evidence that having students practice writing academic essays and research papers in Freshman Writing programs bears almost no relationship to their writing needs across the span of their college life" (Beaufort 2007, 26). Although we learned above that writing courses generate a profit for the department, in times of budget deficits, non-tenure-track faculty and the courses they teach are the easiest to cut. Moreover, this senior professor unknowingly uses the theories of genre and transfer to justify cutting the first-year requirement: since writing specialists themselves say first-year writing courses do not help students in their future courses, it is easier to rationalize cutting this requirement.

TWO ECONOMIES

It should be clear at this point that two different economic logics are structuring higher education institutions: one logic ties prestige to scarcity, and the other logic connects needed services to devaluation. As Marx argued, once a social function is deemed necessary for society, it must be devalued so low wages can be justified. After all, it would be very expensive to pay for the services we all need (like parenting, food service, and cleaning). In contrast, expertise is itself defined as a scarce resource, so the meritocracy feeds a prestige economy in which only a few can succeed.

The conflict between the two economic logics I have discussed above weaves in and out of Beaufort's book, but once she turns her attention to the particular student she is studying, these institutional factors tend to disappear. In one specific passage, she does discuss the dialectic between institutional and instructional processes:

> This discourse community of peers and teacher (and the associated social pressures of meeting expectations of peers and teacher, the power hierarchies, etc.) is not a writing context/ discourse community students would think about consciously or fully in its theoretical or practical manifestations unless there were an overt discussion of the ways the class itself functions as a temporary discourse community within a larger institutional discourse community. But nonetheless, standards for good writing, roles assigned to writers and readers, goals of the course—all of these social dynamics of a course as discourse communities affect writers' motivations, performances, and perceptions and extend the meaning of social context beyond that of a specific addressee for a writing project. Students will determine what to write, how much time to spend on the task, etc. based on their perceptions of the discourse community of the course and their personal motivations in relation to that discourse community. (Beaufort 2007, 34)

Beaufort is correct in stressing that students on their own don't usually think about the larger institutional factors shaping their learning environments, but it is unclear whether she thinks faculty should address these issues directly with their students. After all, if writing is always shaped by its social context, it seems important to discuss these issues with students; however, many faculty resist revealing the economic and political forces affecting the learning environment, and this lack of material considerations often places the production and consumption of knowledge within a decontextualized context in institutions of higher education.[13]

What we must consider is what it would mean if we revealed to students the political economy of knowledge production in higher education. Furthermore, don't we do our students a disservice if we represent teaching and learning as activities separated from larger social and cultural forces? Although Beaufort wants to maintain an apolitical conception of writing expertise, it is hard to imagine how one can completely repress the political. In fact, in Beaufort's and other writing studies texts, the efforts to repress the political economy of higher education constantly fail, so in the symptomatic form of the return of the repressed, irrational institutional factors continue to emerge in displaced ways.[14]

One such eruption of displaced material concerns occurs in the tension Beaufort describes between the student she studies, Tim, and his first-year writing instructor's focus on audience. As his teacher Carla articulates in her syllabus, she wants students to write in a way that feels real and important to them: "The problem with traditional academic writing is that it often feels artificial, an exercise bearing little resemblance either to writing as a real learning process or writing in the 'real' world; academic writing tends to be not a dialogue but a one-way inter-action, a report from the student to the instructor who wields the all-powerful grade. In this course, your readership will be expanded to include your peers as well as people outside the academic community" (37). Here, this non-tenure-track lecturer is pushing her students to think of writing outside the context of grades and academic discourse.[15] Beaufort reports that at the time, Tim enjoyed this newly found freedom to write in a more authentic way, but he later resented this approach when he had to write for other academic courses:

> And because there was no meta-discussion in his writing class of discourse communities or the ways in which standards for writing change in different discourse communities, Tim told me he felt he had "sold out," from what Carla espoused when he wrote for history and later engineering. Tim assumed Carla's principles for what constitutes appropriate ways of writing to be universal norms for good writing. As we shall see . . . he intuitively picked up some differences in writing for history teachers or engineers rather than for Carla, but the boundaries and differences between discourse communities were only hazily recognized through trial and error. (Beaufort 2007, 38)

It appears that Beaufort does indeed blame Carla for not pro-viding a metadiscussion of how writing differs in distinct dis-ciplines and genres and how there is no universal model for writing. However, this conflict brings up several related ques-tions: (1) Is the problem Carla's course or the other courses that do not allow students to write in an authentic way? (2) Can a sustained metadiscourse in a first-year writing course prepare students for all the specific demands of their future courses? (3) Can we blame a teacher when a student fails to understand the changing requirements of new genres? and (4) How does Carla's employment situation affect the ways she teaches and interacts with her students? The answer to these questions are complex and interwoven, but it is essential to continue to think about what should be done if our conceptions of effective teaching and learning conflict with the dominant institutional structures and values.

One of Beaufort's chief concerns about Carla's teaching is the way this instructor stresses rhetoric and style over the content of writing: "I observed several class sessions given over mostly to discussions of the readings, the primary thrust of conversation was around analysis of the writer's rhetorical moves in the selected texts, rather than any debate about the content of the essays" (Beaufort 2007, 39). Later on Beaufort adds, "Carla is urging her students to interact with their subject matter not just at the level of comprehension, but also at the levels of analysis and synthesis. And yet in these discussions, the analysis of the writer's argument is done in a vacuum. The students must judge the work without the benefit of knowing the values, the goals, the ongoing conversations of the discourse community in which the writer was addressing his argument, and without the benefit of a knowledge base regarding the subject of the debate (animal rights)" (42). Here, Beaufort points to an important problem facing most college classes, which is the difference between experts and novices.[16] Although Beaufort wants to focus on the reasons it is hard to write effectively if one does not have expertise in a particular subject, underlying her argument is a developmental meritocratic model, and it is important to remember she sees expertise as an apolitical subject. Thus, her emphasis on particular genres and the ability to master specific course content does not only call into question the universality of first-year writing courses, but it also embraces a universalizing discourse of meritocratic expertise.[17]

Her text is in many ways structured by two conceptions of universality: on the one hand, she privileges particular genres and discourses over general writing skills, and on the other hand, she presents a universalistic model of development. The tension between these two universalities can be found in the following passage:

> I argue that the fine points of an argument and the appropriateness of persuasive moves are best evaluated in the context of a specific subject matter as it is grounded within a particular discourse community. . . . As is often the case in freshman writing courses, in Carla's course other matters take higher priority than the topics read about and written about: managing the writing process, learning new genres or principles for making arguments. Even in a theme-based course such as this one, subject matter can become secondary to writerly concerns in part because the teacher has too many things in the curriculum to juggle and because the role of subject matter in a writer's success or failure at a writing task has been a neglected matter in the field. (Beaufort 2007, 43)

What is contradictory about this approach is that as it generalizes about first-year composition courses, it holds onto the view that particular content determines the essential aspect of a written discourse. One reason for this conflict is that first-year composition courses are often defined as without content because they teach general methods of analysis and writing, and this "lack of content" opens the door for administrators to posit that anyone can teach writing. Yet, I claim there is another alternative: proponents of writing studies can argue that the content of these courses is general writing skills, and these skills can only be taught by highly trained, secure faculty. Instead of trying to mimic the dominant university research paradigm, writing studies should position composition as the defender of undergraduate education, effective pedagogy, secure faculty, and student learning. This strategy entails challenging the institutional hierarchies that privilege research over teaching, faculty over students and tenured faculty over part-time instructors. Not only should these institutional hierarchies be challenged and changed, but we must also question the ways we assess and grade students.

GRADING AND DEGRADING

This need for a different conception of assessment becomes evident if we look at the way grading shapes how and why students write.[18] For example, in her discussion of the key role of genre in college composition, Beaufort stresses that schooling produces the notion that one writes mainly to earn grades: "Genres are the ongoing mechanism of communication for a variety of social purposes: for example, getting a grade or display of knowledge (most school genres), entertaining a reader, moving an audience to action, or the writer's catharsis" (45). This description of school genres presents Beaufort with a central problem: how can she argue writing should be determined by particular discourses while she acknowledges students write for the universal goal of getting a good grade?[19] Moreover, how can students write in a meaningful and authentic way in school if school itself imposes an alienating model of assessment?[20]

This conflict between authentic writing and alienated discourse is apparent when she discusses Carla's teaching methods:

> It is ironic that the assignment Carla conceptualized as the most authentic in terms of "real world" writing, Tim felt the most artificial because he was required to assume the perspective of an organization he felt no particular affinity to. This irony—that the assignment that was to create the most overt sense of audience in fact only fostered rebellion—points to the difficult challenge of students' perceiving writing tasks in school contexts as authentic in any other context and making the appropriate shifts in rhetorical stance. Tim's reaction to this assignment (and to other assignments given by later teachers) was perhaps, in part, because of the contrast with Carla's assignments, which were very open-ended and gave the writer lots of choices for subject matter, genre, and rhetorical purpose. Tim was able to write most of his freshman writing essays in an expressive style, designed to achieve the rhetorical aim of entertaining the reader, which he enjoyed. (Beaufort 2007, 50)

Here, Beaufort is bemoaning the fact that the freedom Carla gave Tim failed to prepare him for his future, alienating writing assignments in other classes. Furthermore, she later questions what effect Carla's teaching and grading had on Tim throughout his academic career: "If Tim was an A+ writer in his second quarter of college according to Carla's standards, what motivation did he have to increase his writing skills in the three and a half years to follow? And not to be ignored is Carla's assessment of his skills with the literary essay: Carla gave high praise but Richard Rodriguez set a higher bar for Tim on that essay" (53). Beaufort appears bothered by the high grade Tim got in Carla's class, and she wonders about how this grade affected his motivations in future classes, but she does not directly confront the many problems grades in general produce in relation to higher education. Like so many educators, she questions the effect of grading on learning as she reinforces the meritocratic structure supporting the grading system.

Beaufort not only thinks Carla gave Tim grades he may not have deserved, but she also believes Carla failed to give Tim enough instruction in detecting the diverse genres he would have to utilize in his other classes:

> Of course, Carla could not train Tim in the fine points of writing in history or writing in engineering. But what if Tim had been introduced to the concept of discourse community and genre and had been invited to view the readings and assignments in freshman writing through those conceptual lenses? What if he had had to analyze the genres he was reading and writing for freshman writing? What if the intellectual content of the course had been more challenging—would his abilities in logic and reasoning have been challenged and strengthened? And can a teacher of writing teach one to write for a discourse community the teacher is not a part of? (Beaufort 2007, 58)

Beaufort's analysis of Carla's teaching here brings up a central issues reoccurring in writing studies research: teachers are faulted for not helping students to be successful writers in their future classes. Even though Carla does not have a secure teaching position, and she is not a writing studies specialist, Beaufort experts her to fundamentally transform her student's perceptions of writing, learning, and discourse communities.[21] Moreover, when Beaufort does describe the role of writing in Tim's other classes, it shows how Carla's attention to his writing represented a rare chance for him to engage in a direct conversation about his own compositions:

> Writing itself was an overt and primary topic of discussion in
> freshman writing but not in history; multiple drafts were expect-
> ed in the writing courses and not in history; and students were
> required in the freshman writing courses to supplement class
> sessions with 1:1 or small group tutorials on writing with the
> writing instructor, whereas in history there was little support for
> writers. Tim told me that he might run an idea for an essay by
> his history TA and that he talked to the history TA after he had
> received feedback on his essay (for the purpose of disputing the
> TA's evaluation of his work) but as far as I could see, there was no
> instruction in writing in his history classes. (Beaufort 2007, 57)

My point here is not to argue that Beaufort underestimates the
quality of Carla's teaching; rather, it is clear that Carla's focus on
Tim's writing represented a rare opportunity for this student to
get direct feedback on his compositions as he wrote about subjects he cared about.

What is then often repressed or not dealt with in a full way in
Beaufort's text is the ongoing battle between learning and earning (grades, credits, degrees). Although it may seem idealistic
and naïve to think we can change the way we assess students, it
is hard to imagine how a writing studies approach to education
can take full effect in a culture in which students are socialized
to care only about the grade they receive for their work. For
instance, in one of Tim's reflections on his writing for other
courses, we see how the process of transfer may be blocked by
the focus on grades: "I could have presented my point better,
but he just disagreed with my conclusion . . . in order to get the
grade on the paper you had to say what you'd been told in class
about the book. Maybe in a new way, maybe in more depth, but
basically say the same thing" (58). On one level, one could say
grading helps the process of transferring the teacher's knowledge
to the students by rewarding conformity to graded content, but
on another level, it is clear Tim internalized the message that it
does not matter what a student thinks: what matters is what the
teacher says will be on the test.

This focus on rewarding student conformity with external
rewards not only undermines the desire for critical thinking,
but it also replaces intrinsic motivation with external tokens.[22]

Perhaps the power of this educational structure is that it trains students to be competitive individualists (capitalists) while it limits social disruption and dissent. From this perspective, the main role of education is to produce competitive and compliant citizens who learn their own ideas do not really matter. Therefore, the underlying logic of assessment presented here through the concepts of transfer and genre points to a neoliberal ideology of compliant meritocracy. For instance, Tim shows he was aware he was being asked to conform to a system in which he did not believe: "It was an exercise in regurgitation. What we could tell we had learned or know. So it wasn't a real paper. I got my A or whatever, which I thought was ridiculous" (Beaufort 2007, 59). In conforming to the expert knowledge of the teacher, this student internalizes the genre of "doing school," but this conformity is performed in a state of self-division: the student is rewarded with an external marker of conformity, but he feels the writing is not real.

The alienating effects of this model of education are revealed in how Tim has a hard time transferring knowledge learned in his writing course to other classes. For instance, in response to the courses he later took in history, Beaufort reflects that the genre of the history essay requires a replacement of personal investment with a more abstract and impersonal style of argumentation: "One senses from the history professors' comments that they desired a greater certitude in students' writing and a more formal essay structure as a result, with the writer placed more in the background, at a distance from the audience. To be credible, in the history classes Tim was taking, it appeared one needed to make a clear-cut argument" (Beaufort 2007, 60). What Beaufort finds lacking in Tim's writing is his inability to conform to the expected genres of particular academic disciplines:

> The TA was asking for an essay that not only fulfilled the subject matter requirements of a history essay, but also one that followed conventions for structure of historical essays. Tim did not understand the TA's feedback in terms of the differing genre expectations for the "essay" within different discourse communities. He interpreted the TA's feedback without understanding of what

was behind the comment—the genre expectations in history that the TA was using. (Beaufort 2007, 62)

For Beaufort, the key point here appears to be that writing classes must prepare students to master the various genres they will encounter in their other courses, yet her theory of transfer, which is based on a model of expertise, tells us novice students will never be able to master particular discourses if they don't first master the knowledge and writing expectations required by a particular discipline. The student is then placed in an impossible position of having to write like an expert without experiencing a full immersion in a particular discourse community. Moreover, this process of gaining expertise through sustained experience is undermined by the constant push to replace learning with grading: "From all appearances, the primary rhetorical situation (with the exception of Tim's community service project in freshman writing) in both classes was writing for the teacher and the grade. In freshman writing, Tim had a sense of an appreciative, interested audience in his teacher. In history, he felt quite removed from the teacher as audience for his writing" (Beaufort 2007, 63). One of the conflicts exposed here is that students are being asked to act as if they are real members of a particular discourse community, but the grading system creates an alienating relationship between the student and the main representative of the expert discourse—the teacher.

Instead of focusing on the destructive nature of the grading culture, Beaufort argues that this student saw everything in terms of testing because he did not understand the particular genre he was being asked to replicate: "Tim was not primed by teachers in either discourse community to understand different values and community purposes as they would affect writing goals, content, structure, language choice, rhetorical situation, etc. Tim's view that his history professors were trying to get him to agree with their points of view was probably caused by Tim's not understanding the requirements for supporting arguments in the discourse community of historians" (Beaufort 2007, 65). While Tim is faulted for not picking up on the particularities of specific writing situations, the teachers are also critiqued for not communicating the discrete genre considerations needed so one can be considered an expert in a particular discourse.

One reason Tim may not have gotten the genre knowledge he needed in his nonwriting courses is that his TAs and professors did not teach this aspect of the discourse: "Was there any explicit instruction in how to approach writing tasks? Tim reported only one such instance: in his colonial American history class the professor gave some guidance on how to do an in-depth rhetorical analysis of a primary source" (Beaufort 2007, 99). It is thus hard to imagine how this student could have learned to write in more appropriate ways for particular genres if his teachers did not teach him how to do this or even how to think about genres. Therefore, a key problem for transfer and genre is that many classes outside first-year writing courses are taught by people who do not know or understand the fundamental principles of writing studies.

Although writing is often not taught in nonwriting classes, and if it is, it is often taught by people with limited training and expertise in writing studies, Beaufort reports that faculty from other programs still expect students to be effective writers:

> One engineering faculty member told me that those on the industry board for his department say they hire engineers first for ability to work well with others, and second, for communications skills. Industry members say that they can train new engineers in technical skills; the other two skills they need to have when they finish school. Another board member told the engineering faculty member, "If a graduate of your school wrote incorrect sentences, I'd fire him and not hire another graduate from your school for a long time." (Beaufort 2007, 104)

It is interesting that employers and faculty expect a certain level of writing fluency, but writing is still often held in low esteem by many academic institutions.[23] Of course, one reason for this problem is that employers and faculty outside writing often have a limited definition of writing—grammatical correctness—so they do not see the many different rhetorical and cognitive aspects of composition.

From Beaufort's perspective, what prevents students from being able to adjust to different writing genres is that they do not have the sustained experience of using these forms in real practice. The paradox of transfer here is that one can only learn how to write like an insider by being an insider, but being an insider is not possible within a school setting, so it is unclear whether writing can be taught in higher education at all:

> Winsor found that students mimicked the language of the models for reports, without understanding the rhetorical import of that language. In a follow-up study (Winsor 1999), when the students were now employees of the engineering firm, Winsor found that their understanding of purposes for writing (for example, to document actions and protect themselves from possible recriminations) increased. (Beaufort 2007, 108)

If students can only really learn how to write for specific situations by being immersed in these institutions, the whole artificial nature of school works against transfer.

The difficult problem of transfer and genre in writing studies may be the result of not taking into full consideration the general habits of mind and the basic writing skills that can be taught in a first-year writing course. Instead of seeing failure when students do not learn how to enter into specific expert discourses, it may be important to return to the general skills and principles that can be taught in a series of writing courses, like grammatical correctness, rhetorical awareness, critical analysis, and argument coherence. Students will never become expert writers in a particular domain unless they are exposed to the discourse community on a real and ongoing basis, so it may be that aspects of the theory of genre lead us in the wrong direction.

What many people inside and outside academic institutions often discount are the fundamental habits of mind derived from the modern university. The stress on being logical, rational, empirical, neutral, methodological, and objective emphasizes and values dispositions that are not natural; rather, these dispositions are socially constructed and must be taught and maintained. However, these habits of mind can be undermined by the use of grades and assessment, just as science itself can be corrupted if it is driven by individualistic or monetary concerns. Unfortunately, even at research universities, the ethics and rationale of the modern scientific mindset are rarely taught or discussed in a direct way, and without an understanding of this ethical foundation for academic discourse, it is easy to dismiss academic writing as an artificial mode of composition with no value outside itself. For instance, when Beaufort compares the writing Tim did in school with the writing he did in his engineering job, she tends to privilege the value of the work discourse community over the university discourse: "Given the constraints of the social context in school, however, Tim had limited opportunities to learn the intricacies of the rhetorical situations he would encounter in the workplace. It is also worth noting that he separated the critical thinking part of the school projects from the writing, the former being the 'real work' and the latter just an obligatory function of being in school and the professor needing something to grade" (129). Instead of setting up oppositions between school and work and writing and critical thinking, it might be more helpful to look at how composition courses can provide opportunities for the development of important thinking and writing skills that can be used inside and outside the classroom, and yet the social role played by grading continues to block this type of education.

Beyond the problems caused by the need to assess and sort students, and the emphasis students put on conforming to educational expectations, the writing studies concept of transfer as presented in Beaufort's study often suffers from a conflict over two different conceptions of teaching genre in a writing course. Her most common view is that students can only really learn how to write a specific genre by being immersed in an actual social situation that requires this type of communication, yet she also at times turns to a less extreme interpretation of genre and transfer: "I would argue that we are looking to teach not similarities in the ways writing is done in different contexts, but rather, to teach those broad concepts (discourse community, genre, rhetorical tools, etc.) which will give writers the tools to analyze similarities and differences among writing situations they encounter" (Beaufort 2007, 145). This second theory of genre does point toward teaching generalizable skills in a first-year writing course because students are trained how to look for specific communicative features not tied to particular expertise knowledge.

Ultimately, Beaufort is right to call for the teaching of genres in all disciplines and levels of higher education, but the question remains, how can nonexpert faculty teach students key aspects of writing studies if the teachers themselves are not experts in this field? Beaufort does not deal with this issue, but she does turn to a more achievable and generalizable notion of genre and transfer when she examines teaching writing outside the composition classroom:

> Lower and upper division courses and even graduate courses should be accompanied, no matter what the discipline, by a sequence of writing tasks for students to undertake that will gradually increase the challenges in the tasks assigned and move students along in critical areas of writing expertise: discourse community goals and values, genre conventions in the community, and interpretive/critical thinking skills that are necessary companions to subject matter, rhetorical skills, and writing process skills. The data presented here point to this need for continuity of writing instruction across the college curriculum. (Beaufort 2007, 150)

Unfortunately, in order to accomplish this level of writing instruction, a university or college would not only need expert faculty but also small classes and a new model of assessment.

Although one would hope Beaufort would make a call for teachers to become experts in writing studies, she actually blames faculty autonomy for the lack of progress in teaching genre and transfer: "Even within composition studies, there is not enough emphasis on developing curricular sequences across writing courses. Teacher autonomy should not be the primary criterion for curricular decisions when students' developmental progress is at stake" (Beaufort 2007, 151). While it may be true that we should not let faculty autonomy undermine the implementation of an effective educational initiative, it is unfair to blame faculty for the structural and institutional barriers limiting the type of pedagogy called for by writing studies. As Beaufort's own work shows, the practices called for by writing studies research will only be possible if a different type of university is invented.

NOTES

1. For a critique of Beaufort's methodology, see Taber (2010).
2. See Janice M. Lauer (1984).
3. Extended analysis of the relation between grading and meritocracy can be found in Kohn (2000) and Michael Young (1958).
4. See Smit (2004).
5. For an interesting discussion of the universal and near-universal aspects of composition, see Mohan and Lo (1985).
6. Denise Pope (2001) offers an insightful analysis of how schools train students to only focus on grades as they go through the motions of pretending to learn.
7. An explanation of habits of mind can be found in Costa and Kallick (2009).
8. For an analysis of some of the problems facing courses that teach how to write in specific disciplines, see Barbara E. Walvoord (1996).
9. Žižek (1989) argues that one of the most dominant forms of ideology is the claim that one is outside ideology and politics.
10. The conservative discourse of color blindness is deconstructed in John Powell (2008).
11. Christopher Hayes (2013) provides an insightful critique of meritocracy.
12. See Bousquet (2008).
13. Victor Villanueva (2001) has pushed for a more material understanding of writing studies.
14. One defining aspect of our current neoliberal culture is the backlash against social criticism and the postmodern analysis of race, class, and gender. On many levels, we can see writing studies as participating in this reactionary discourse.
15. At the end of her book, Beaufort does give Carla a chance to talk back, and the result is that many of Beaufort's interpretations of this teacher's practices are called into question.
16. Although Beaufort wants composition instructors to focus on content, many proponents of writing studies see a focus on content as a distraction from the writing process and rhetorical analysis. For analysis of this debate over content in composition, see Lisa Bosley (2008).
17. For a critique of education-based meritocracy, see Stuart Tannock (2008).
18. For a general critique of writing see Kohn (2000).
19. David Labaree (2012) has presented a convincing argument about how grading affects all levels of education.

20. David Bartholomae (1985) presents an ambivalent analysis of how students are forced to conform to alienating standards in his "Inventing the University." *The Politics of Writing Studies* can be read as in dialogue with this earlier text.

21. One of the most troubling aspects of the neoliberal take on education is the idea that the teacher is the main source for student progress. According to this ideology, bad teachers should be easily fired since they determine the future earnings of their students. Moreover, in order to allow the best teachers to rise to the top, one must eliminate unions, tenure, and seniority considerations. This very argument was the foundation a California Supreme Court decision (Vergara v. State of California) that stated that tenure was unconstitutional.

22. For an extensive critique of grading and external rewards, see Kohn (2000).

23. Adler-Kassner and O'Neill (2010) discuss how writing is misunderstood both inside and outside higher education.

3

METACOGNITION AND CYNICAL CONFORMITY IN *WRITING ACROSS CONTEXTS*

Writing across Contexts: Transfer, Composition, and Cultures of Writing by Kathleen Blake Yancey, Liane Robertson, and Kara Taczak offers a close examination of the ways the writing studies concepts of transfer, genre, and metacognition help us focus on what prevents students from applying new knowledge to different situations (Yancey, Robertson, and Taczak 2014). Their overall claim is that if students learn to use key concepts from writing studies to become more self-aware about how they write, they will be better able to adapt writing strategies to new contexts. From this perspective, self-knowledge can overcome institutional and cultural constraints. Yet, they also reveal the ways the teaching of college writing is always affected by the type of schooling and socialization that occurs before students enter into higher education. This dialectic between past and present knowledge results in an ambivalent structure in which self-knowledge is seen as the key to overcoming social and structural limitations, but these same cultural forces also shape the self and the knowledge one has of the self. Moreover, self-reflection can provide the illusion that we can overcome political and economic constraints by simply adapting to them in a self-aware way.[1]

As I argue in the previous chapters, writing studies is threatened by its ambivalent relationship with the material realities shaping higher education and the neoliberal political economy. On one level, we find careful attention to the problems posed by the devaluing of writing, teaching, and undergraduate students in a system that privileges research, theory, and graduate education; however, since people do not think we can change the current hierarchies, the only option is to find ways to conform to

DOI: 10.7330/9781607325840.c003

the system from a perspective of critical distance. In this chapter, we will see how the writing studies concept of metacognition may lead to another way of conforming to a discredited system through the idealization of educational self-awareness.

THE K–12 EFFECT

Throughout their book, Yancey, Robertson, and Taczak do pay attention to how the dominant structures of K–12 education do not prepare students for college writing. In fact, students are often constrained by the way high-school classes have socialized them to only write for grades.[2] For example, one of the students they study can be considered a victim of her own precollege writing success:

> Emma pursued a two-part strategy imported from high school—avoiding error and meeting teachers' expectations—that resulted in a kind of school-success. . . . Emma's approach to writing throughout the two terms was framed doubly: (1) correctness, in particular through the "rules for correctness" she had learned in high school, and (2) the meeting of teacher expectations for each assignment. In her mind the two were linked, as she explains: "I do like choosing what I write about as long as I have specific guidelines to write on. I like to know what I'm being graded on and what the criteria is. That way I can't do anything wrong." Emma's definition of writing didn't change during the two terms, especially since her approach to writing was consistently rewarded all the way up the food chain by good grades in all three contexts: high school; FYC; and the courses she took in the post-composition semester. (Yancey, Robertson, and Taczak 2014, 77)

As this passage reveals, it may be hard to get students to write and think in a different way if they have been rewarded in the past for conforming to a narrow notion of effective writing. In short, if we want students to be creative and critical writers, we must find some way of changing their learned behaviors.

The power of high-school education to shape the way students approach college writing is presented in the following passage about the same "successful" student:

She transferred what she had learned about writing in high school—that is, her writing knowledge, captured in her perception of the role of error in writing and the need to avoid it—to her college composition course. Moreover, in responding to her post-composition writing requirements, rather than calling on her FYC experience, Emma "leapfrogs" her writing knowledge from high school over the FYC context as she takes up post-composition writing assignments. In one humanities course, for example, Emma was required to write about gender representation in film by looking at the work of a specific director. Emma approached this assignment by drawing on other writing knowledge, what she knew about writing high school literary analyses, as she explains: "I've done analysis since high school, so it was no big deal. I did it like an analysis of a piece of literature, only it was film, and just followed the specific format. And the research we did was like we learned in high school and in 1102 [the second term of the two-term sequence], so I knew where to go to look at the databases, or to just Google the director." Drawing on her knowledge of literary analysis to write in the context of film, Emma engages in near transfer as defined by Perkins and Salomon (1992), moving from one context to another without consciously realizing that she is considering the differences in situation and material. (Yancey, Robertson, and Taczak 2014, 78)

Due to her strong background and success in her high-school English courses, this student appears to be unaffected by her college writing class, and thus she employs composing and analysis methods she learned before higher education in her college courses. Here, it is clear transfer has failed because it is being blocked by a previous form of socialization.[3] It is therefore hard to imagine how a college composition course can help students break from their previous writing strategies, especially if these techniques were highly rewarded.

One reason some students may complain that they learn nothing in their required college composition courses is that they resist replacing past methods if those methods earned them praise and high grades: "She doesn't identify writing knowledge from her college writing course as helpful—even though both the college and the high school class shared some of the same practices and thus some of the same content—because she cannot identify any content from FYC that might apply, other than

Googling for information. In a very common sense way, what Emma can identify as applicable—her high school knowledge of the genre of literary analysis and how to compose one—is what she transfers" (78). Part of the issue here is the idea that students can only learn something new if they are willing to see themselves as novices, but if they have been highly rewarded for their past actions, there is no reason for them to view themselves as beginners:

> Emma doesn't see herself as a novice, in the Sommers and Saltz (2004) sense, because her college writing assignments don't ask her to be one. Perhaps, then, it was not surprising that her theory about writing that she shared in her penultimate interview echoed what she had said as she entered FYC: avoid error, please the teacher—in her words, "appease the teacher"—and, if possible, connect empathetically with the teacher for feedback: "Talking to my teacher and going over my paper with her was always a plus also." (Yancey, Robertson, and Taczak 2014, 78)

It appears that this student has learned very well how to "do school," which means she is good at conforming to the expectations of the system and appeasing authority figures; however, this type of conformity does not help her learn new ways of writing or applying new knowledge to novel situations.[4]

In studying what knowledge students transfer from one situation to the next, it is important to examine both the negative and positive aspects of using past knowledge in new contexts. In fact, the following example shows a student being both helped and hindered by previous writing courses:

> For example, in describing the genre of his physics lab reports, he noted similarities to and differences from his writing in a humanities context. The physics lab report, he explained, "required a step-by-step description of the lab process and plenty of math, plus drawings, if necessary," and he commented that the purpose of writing was "to understand the properties of light and sound." This purpose, he noted, was similar to the writing in his humanities course, where the goal "was also to show understanding of the subject matter, but also to analyze the works of important figures and see how they relate." Thus, Glen saw both similarities and differences in the writing of the two situations.

> On the other hand, Glen sometimes projected more similarity
> between two writing sites than was actually the case, especially
> when, to him, they seemed to be "naturally" similar. In fact, he
> expected connections between the writing in first-year composi-
> tion and his post-FYC humanities course, and here his expecta-
> tion, at least in part, set him up for an unsuccessful experience,
> or failure. (Yancey, Robertson, and Taczak 2014, 79)

Since in college, students write for many different courses
and disciplines, they must be adept at detecting what genre
is demanded by particular contexts, but students often fail at
adapting because they are locked into a single way of writing,
which is often learned in high school or a first-year composition course: "Basically, his approach to the assignment relied
on replicating prior experiences—compiling information and
presenting it in an FYC-type research essay (as he had experi-
enced it)—rather than on repurposing or developing a new or
adaptive strategy to write in what was in fact a new genre, the
fully researched and synthetic humanities analysis connecting
ideas from multiple contexts" (80). Thus, while we often hear
first-year writing courses do not prepare students for the different classes they take throughout their college careers, the theories of transfer and genre tell us it is impossible to teach college
writing in a single class because there is no single way of writing
in college. The theory of metacognition then tries to rectify this
situation by arguing that we can at least teach students to understand different genre demands and to self-consciously adjust
their writing to new contexts.[5]

Part of the problem of transfer thus revolves around the fact
that the faculty in other disciplines do not often focus on how
to write and think differently in their particular domains. For
instance, in large lecture classes, professors often deliver knowledge as if it is objective, neutral, and universal, and thus the production and communication of this discourse need not be compared and contrasted with other disciplines.[6] Therefore, just as
high school socializes students to write in a particular way, college
courses often expect students to adjust to different genres at the
same time the disciplines see their discourse as being universal.

As the authors of *Writing across Contexts* point out, it is not only the style and form of writing that changes according to specific disciplines, but the whole approach to knowledge is often different. First-year writing courses are therefore in a bind if people expect them to prepare students for writing in any field since each field not only requires different writing genres but also different epistemologies. This conflict is evident in the following student example:

> Nor did Glen consider the rhetorical situation of the humanities assignment, especially the broader social perspective of the context in which his humanities course's discussions on morality were based. Instead, perhaps misled by the similarities between this assignment and the FYC assignments, he reverted to the writer-centered approach informed by the values of imagery and interesting narrative from the content of the FYC course. In other words, Glen employed the specific writing techniques he learned in FYC, which focused more on expressing oneself as a writer, rather than on writing an effective and rhetorically objective analysis. Thus, although Glen did transfer writing knowledge he learned in FYC, it was not writing knowledge that was appropriate to the new context. Glen's grade on the humanities essay was an unpleasant surprise to him, but it also prompted him to approach writing differently. (Yancey, Robertson, and Taczak 2014, 79)

The problem here is not only that this student tried to write a literary essay in a nonliterary course but also that he did not understand the difference in methodologies, key concepts, and theories. Writing studies is therefore presented with the difficult problem of trying to prepare students for classes that have very distinct forms and content.

Although I do not think any class or discipline can prepare students for all other disciplines, what is clear is that writing studies can help other disciplines to improve their teaching by making learning much more dialogical. From this perspective, faculty must realize they need to engage students in a conversation about the previous knowledge students bring into new learning situations.[7] We can see this need for dialogue in the following example: "After his humanities essay was returned, Glen reported that his professor talked to him about expectations for analysis in writing, and it was in that conversation that Glen realized that the context was different than it had been in the FYC course" (Yancey, Robertson, and Taczak 2014, 80). In other words, if teachers do not speak with their students about what the students know and expect, it is hard for the teachers to help students learn since old knowledge is blocking new learning.

CAN METACOGNITION SAVE THE UNIVERSITY?

The type of education I am calling for here of course is in conflict with many of the current modes of teaching in higher education, so it unclear how the writing studies notion of transfer can really be used in an effective manner if it requires a type of explicit knowledge and teaching not common today. Yet, the authors of *Writing across Contexts* still believe the right kind of first-year composition course could actually prepare students for better writing and learning in future courses:

> The content of this first-year composition course, then, did not support transfer for Emma and Glen, and in two ways. First, since it did not provide the opportunity for students to develop a broader set of terms for writing, or a conceptual writing framework, they had no passport with which to transition from FYC to other contexts. Second, while the Expressivist course included the practice of reflection, it did not engage students in using reflection to theorize . . . put simply, reflection functioned in practice as a process addendum to writing assignments rather than as a source of invention for understanding writing. In sum, without an explicit theoretical construct of writing organizing and anchoring the course, course content was not supporting these students as they took on new writing assignments. (Yancey, Robertson, and Taczak 2014, 82)

The argument here is that if students learned a more explicit theory of writing in their first-year writing class, they would be better able to transfer their knowledge to new classes and contexts; in other words, instead of changing the way the other classes are taught, we must prepare students in a single class to become more self-conscious about how they learn.

The analogy that comes to mind for this argument is Descartes's idea that since the only thing we really control is our own thoughts, even a prisoner can be free if they just imagine their life in a different way. Although students are not prisoners, they are part of larger systems, and these structures often reward specific forms of behavior, yet in the context of higher education, there is still the idea that there is a standard, universal way of thinking, reading, and writing. Moreover, since people do not believe we can afford an educational system that actually engages students in a dialogue over what they do and do not know, everyone pretends effective learning can still occur in ineffective learning structures. The push for metacognition then might by another way of ignoring material constraints by offering an abstract intellectual solution.

The authors of *Writing across Contexts* do a good job of pointing to all the ways students' internalization of educational structures block their learning and writing, yet they continue to argue that if students just learn the right vocabulary and theories, they will be able to adjust to every new situation:

> Without a curriculum explicitly based on a writing vocabulary or set of key terms, students often leave the classroom unsure of what they did learn; they then leapfrog to earlier knowledge and practice that may be more or less helpful, rather than employing a writing-rich language model of curriculum as an approach to understanding and responding to new writing situations. Key terms, fully conceptualized and reiteratively learned and used in the classroom, offer students a vocabulary with which they can articulate learned writing knowledge and which is available for use in other rhetorical situations. (Yancey, Robertson, and Taczak 2014, 101)

The core idea here is that if students learn the key concepts, terms, and theories of writing studies in a self-reflective manner, they will be able to transfer knowledge to new situations in an effective way. Part of this theory rests on the idea that students need the right words to express what they are learning: "In sum, such a vocabulary contributes to the passport students need to transition to new contexts. Without such a language, students cannot easily describe individual writing tasks or similarities and differences across them; without such a language, borders to these new worlds represented by new ways of writing and thinking too often remain closed to them" (Yancey, Robertson, and Taczak 2014, 101). Although I would not argue against the idea that students may benefit from having a more conscious understanding of how they write in different contexts, there is a risk that writing studies faculty may be overly impressed by students who are able to repeat back to their teachers the expected discourse.[8] In other words, since we have already seen how good some students are at giving teachers what the students think the teachers want, it would not be surprising if the interviewed students are simply conforming to educational expectations.

In what has been called *cynical conformity*, our society often rewards people who comply with social expectations even if this compliance is done with irony and disengagement.[9] In fact, one could argue that the essential skill schools teach is cynical conformity because students are rewarded for compliance through grades even though the students often communicate directly and indirectly that they do not care about what they are learning. Likewise, universities reject the value of college rankings as they pour money into increasing their rankings' status.[10] Universities also use ineffective teaching methods and structures even though they know there are better ways of educating people, and these schools also assess many of their faculty with student evaluations even though the universities know these are not statistically valid and may cause grade inflation and defensive teaching.[11] An example of this type of cynical conformity can be seen in the discussion of how some students self-report using the key terms from writing studies but show no evidence of improving their writing:

> Still, despite her comparatively sophisticated understanding of audience and purpose, and despite the course design, Marta did not employ or think in terms of the key terms linking assignments in the TFT course. While she was able to define the concepts required in the first assignment—genre, audience, and rhetorical situation—she did not recognize those concepts as operating in the second or third assignments. When prompted,

she acknowledged that rhetorical situation was a consideration for the third assignment, but she did not understand it as a requirement for it. In other words, she understood the concepts in the course, including that of rhetorical situation—and at the end of the semester she listed rhetorical situation as one of the key terms in the course—but she did not incorporate the idea of rhetorical situation as a way to think about or frame a writing task. Instead, like her colleagues in the two other versions of FYC, Marta's focus remained on the process of writing rather than on a theoretically informed practice of writing. She discussed the techniques that enhanced her process, specifically in the areas of outlining and revising, but her fundamental writing process did not change, and she did not allow a theory about writing to inform her writing and thinking practices, at least during the scope of this study. (Yancey, Robertson, and Taczak 2014, 89)

I cite this passage at length because it challenges many of the central claims of *Writing across Contexts*. Thus, this student does appear to learn the terms and concepts the instructors feel are necessary for effective metacognition and transfer, but she does not apply this knowledge to new situations. This disconnect between her knowledge and her actions forces us to question whether teachers should ever be evaluated based on the quality of their students' work. Since so much of a student's learning depends on psychology and socialization, it seems unfair to expect teachers to be able to transform the ways students think, read, and learn in a single class or even a series of classes.[12]

The authors of *Writing across Contexts* are forced into a contradictory discourse because they want to push the idea that teaching students about metacognition, transfer, and genre in a writing course can help them transfer new knowledge into new contexts, but the authors can't help but notice all the ways prior knowledge and attitudes shape how students learn: "Put more generally, a significant factor in all the case studies that we didn't appreciate until we began examining the data was the influence of prior knowledge on several dimensions of students' writing experiences: their attitudes toward writing; the strategies they drew upon; the knowledge about writing contextualizing their practices and, consequently, their development as writers" (Yancey, Robertson, and Taczak 2014, 103). It is important to stress that all of these psychological dispositions are also social and institutional formations derived from the educational reward system, and as K–12 becomes increasingly dominated by sorting, grading, testing, and ranking, students are socialized to see writing as a universal form dedicated to proving knowledge and grammatical correctness on standardized tests.[13] While students respond to this structure in different ways, the system still dominates and controls expectations concerning writing and learning.

The socialization of students by their K–12 education is often reinforced by higher education through the use of tests, grades, large lecture classes, and rankings. Thus, even if composition faculty teach students complex and effective methods of writing, these methods may not be supported by other classes. We see this conflict in the following discussion of how some students don't value what they learn in their first-year composition courses:

> However, she also believed that the amount of process writing was too extensive, especially since she did not see its relevance to writing in other courses. Darren expressed the same view: the process requirements, involving multiple drafts, peer reviews, and a process memo, were tedious. In particular, because they perceived the amount of writing in the course as randomly decided and designed to make students work hard rather than help them, Carolina and Darren questioned the need for more than two drafts. As Darren continued classes in the post-composition semester, he noted that he could see no similarities between the FYC course and the writing he did in other courses, but he, like Glen, saw connections between post-composition courses and his high school English classes. (Yancey, Robertson, and Taczak 2014, 83)

Since the college courses in other disciplines did not require these students to revise their writing, it is possible the writing they did in high school was more similar to the writing required in noncomposition college courses than the type of writing asked for in first-year composition courses:

> Given this context, it's not surprising that Darren believed there was nothing he learned in the composition course that was applicable to writing in any other context: "Everything I learned about writing, I learned in high school." In the sense that it was in high school that he learned about types of analysis, basic

research protocols, and grammar, Darren's account is, of course, accurate. Darren also explained that the techniques he learned in the composition course did not fit with his writing style because he doesn't plan or outline, and much as the students in the Bergmann and Zepernick (2007) study, he described a view of FYC process as one at odds with the values of writing in his other courses, where process is either not expected or extra-curricular, in the sense that students are assumed to be completing whatever processes they choose to employ outside of class. Darren thus perceived the extensive, multi-draft process of the FYC course as content, or partial content, that was not as important as the content he learned in other classes. Since he could not articulate the FYC content, he struggled to understand what it was, filling in the writing process as the content he could not otherwise discern. Further, because the writing process was so explicitly elaborate in the FYC course, he perceived it as irrelevant to writing in other courses, as the writing there was dominated by clearly communicated subject matter and nonexistent or implied process. He explains: "It's entirely different. In 1102, your grade is dependent on being able to do things the way other people want you to do them. Content really doesn't matter too much in that class, although it is somewhat important. In other classes, the grade is almost completely dependent on content. In other classes you can write any way that you want as long as the final result is good. 1102 is about the process; other classes are about the product." Carolina's perception of the differences in writing in FYC and in other classes matched Darren's: "The writing in other classes is really simple, or factual, or explanatory. As long as you understand the information you are writing about and explain it clearly through your writing you will do well." She viewed FYC as focused on unnecessary process rather than on the end result; in particular, she didn't understand the logic of the amount of process. (Yancey, Robertson, and Taczak 2014, 85)

Since most other college courses do not focus on writing or student expression, the students often feel their first-year writing courses have no real value, but this problem may say more about the other classes than it says about the first-year composition course.

Instead of addressing the conflict between the teaching methods and value of first-year composition courses and non-writing courses, the authors of *Writing across Contexts* tend to focus on the ways the teachers and the curriculum are not sufficiently explicit and self-conscious: "Without the coherence of an explicit course design integrating relevant assignments, large and small, students were confused about course content, goals, and concepts that might transfer. Accordingly, when Darren and Carolina take up new postcomposition tasks, like McCarthy's (1987) Dave, all they see is difference" (88). Here the concept of transfer is being used to question the value of composition courses that do not take advantage of the latest research in writing studies:

> Perhaps what we have documented here is simply the function of good teaching; better teachers, one might say, help students develop as writers in ways others do not. Were this the case, then this study would be more properly focused on pedagogy. But while the teaching of these three classes doesn't distinguish them one from the next, the attention to curriculum and kinds of curriculum do. (Yancey, Robertson, and Taczak 2014, 99)

The idea here is that it is not so much the teacher who determines the possibilities for successful transfer; instead, it is the curriculum that makes learning possible. One risk of this argument is that it feeds into the idea that anyone can teach writing if they are just given the right preestablished curriculum. In fact, the authors point out that none of the teachers of the classes they examined were actually faculty trained in writing studies: "Each of these FYC courses—the Expressivist approach, the media and culture themed, and the TFT design—had by definition 'good' teachers, and all were graduate students" (Yancey, Robertson, and Taczak 2014, 100). This reliance on graduate-student instructors is never addressed in the study, and in fact, the authors seem to justify the lack of tenured professionals by arguing that the teacher is not as important as the theory:

> Good teaching, though, does not necessarily guarantee that students learn what they need to learn in a course. As noted by Bergmann and Zepernick (2007), even with the best of intentions and years of experience, instructors are not always able to provide students with knowledge about writing they can then use to frame new writing tasks. It is fair to note, however, that some

factors might make a difference, among them the amount of teaching experience of instructors and their educational background, especially if the background, as is the case for rhetoric and composition and writing courses, is directly relevant to the course in question. What we observed in this study was consistent: students looking for identifiable content regardless of course design; and students using the content they could identify—in the case of Emma and Glen, content from high school, and in the case of Clay and Rick, content from the TFT course—to assist them as they approached new writing tasks. In this analysis, then, where the quality of the teaching seems similar, the distinguishing factor isn't the teaching, but rather the curriculum. Moreover, even in a course designed to assist transfer, and in which some students demonstrated successful transfer, others may not transfer due to various factors not related to the quality of teaching, as was the case for Marta. In this regard, what this study suggests—and as was suggested earlier by Hilgers, Hussey, and Stitt-Bergh (1999), Jarratt et al. (2005), and Reiff and Bawarshi (2011)—is that students need a vocabulary for writing in order to articulate knowledge and ensure more successful transfer. (Yancey, Robertson, and Taczak 2014, 101)

There is a lot going on in this passage, but one thing for sure is that when the authors start to move toward recognizing the institutional constraints put on teaching, they affirm that given the right vocabulary and theory, students can overcome material obstacles, yet they remain aware of how prior schooling does affect the ability of students to learn: "We theorize that students progress, or not, relative to their past performances as writers—not so much relative to their experiences as writers, but rather as they have found themselves represented as writers by others, through external benchmarks like grades and test scores. Second, we learned that students often find themselves entering college courses with an absence of prior knowledge, that is, a dearth of information or experience that would be helpful as they begin writing in college" (Yancey, Robertson, and Taczak 2014, 104). As much as the theorists of writing studies try to argue learning can be enhanced without changing basic educational structures, they cannot escape the social, political, and economic realities shaping students' learning environments.

One place it is clear that politics and education policy affect college writers is in the use of advanced placement courses and tests:

> Although national policy rewards students for completing AP courses and earning a high score on the culminating AP test, research suggests that students who identify as AP writers are less likely to see themselves as novice writers when they enter college (Hansen et al. 2004). Likewise, as Tinberg and Nadeau (2011, 2013) explain in both "Contesting the Space between High School and College in the Era of Dual- Enrollment" and "What Happens When High School Students Write in a College Course? A Study of Dual Credit," students coming into college with an experience that pretends to substitute for the college experience are often not as prepared as they believe, and thus are not ready to "benefit in the college classroom" (Tinberg and Nadeau 2011, 704). As one student told us: It's funny how your high school advisors tell you the advantages of taking fourteen A.P. and I.B. courses, but they don't tell you how severely constricting coming into college with 39 credits is. . . . I, the first year sophomore, was positive that I could walk into college and take easy courses because I was just so damn prepared. The students profiled here had a bimodal reaction to the high school experiences constituting their point of departure. On the one hand, for some students the experience was positive and contributed to a strong writer identity, which in some cases—ironically—translated into an unwillingness to learn or explore. These students exhibited (as we saw in chapter 1) what Reiff and Bawarshi (2011) call boundary guarding and what Wardle (2012) conceptualizes as problem solving behavior. On the other hand, for some students the high school experience was a negative one, but it motivated students to try new approaches. These students exhibited a willingness—in Reiff and Bawarshi terminology—to boundary-cross, and in Wardle's—to problem-explore. (Yancey, Robertson, and Taczak 2014, 106)

AP courses and tests not only allow some students to pass out of taking required first-year writing courses, but the use of AP credits can also signal to students that they have nothing to learn from a writing class since they have already been certified as good writers. Moreover, the very idea that you can test out of a writing course sends the message that these classes are only for the students who were unable to master certain skills before college.

Ironically, one of the main concepts students are often taught in their first-year composition course is the reason they need to move beyond the five-paragraph essay structure they learned in high school, and thus the students who were successful in their high-school AP classes and tests may be the ones who need to take first-year composition courses the most:

> Andy, a first-year student majoring in political science, entered the TFT course believing he had been "brainwashed" with the five paragraph assignments teachers use to prepare students for the Florida standardized writing exam, the Florida Comprehensive Assessment Test, or FCAT. He felt "uneasy" about writing generally, and it's probably not surprising since he had no composing process to call on. Because the totality of Andy's writing instruction had been test-specific, he had developed no composing method other than an abbreviated process attuned to the test environment. Upon entering FYC, he attempted to use the single approach he had relied on in high school, writing up an assignment in an hour. This approach to writing, as Scherff and Piazza (2005) discovered, is common for 90% of high school students in Florida. Not surprisingly, as Andy entered college he felt unprepared and ill-equipped for the process approach that was expected and didn't understand what it was, but by the conclusion of the TFT course Andy observed that he had not experienced a "real" writing course until coming to Florida State. For Andy, the FCAT writing test was a point of departure: his "unease" combined with the instruction he received at FSU helped him understand and practice writing very differently than before. (Yancey, Robertson, and Taczak 2014, 107)

The fact that the state requires students to write in this formulaic fashion shows we cannot remove the teaching of writing from politics. Since states are concerned that their students are not learning enough, they have ramped up their use of tests, which then forces schools and teachers to conform to a system few people think is right and effective.[14] Here, cynical conformity is demanded by the entire system, so it should be no surprise if students enter college with a contradictory approach to learning and writing.

This political focus on testing is connected to the way students experience their education in relation to the grades they receive:

Without their own standards for assessing their work, students participating in this study were also especially sensitive to grades. Grades, or the approval of the instructor, led the students to see writing dichotomously, as either good or bad, and to see themselves similarly, as writers whose identities as either "good writers" or "bad writers" were fixed and unchangeable. Darren and Emma . . . believed they were involved in a kind of game of playing up to teachers, not only to meet teacher expectations, but also to project that they cared, that they were concerned about expectations. Both Darren and Emma follow what they perceive to be one of the rules of school: find out what the instructor wants and then write in a way that meets those expectations. For both students, this idea—discover expectations, deliver expectations—had emerged through the success of their method in each local writing context: delivering what they perceive as the marks of good writers, which is rewarded with good grades, and which then confirms their sense that, indeed, they are good writers across contexts. With such powerful experiences of successful writing, it's not surprising that a student wouldn't want to change. (Yancey, Robertson, and Taczak 2014, 107)

This passage does a good job of depicting the ways the testing and grading structures of education shape students' perceptions about their own learning and how to succeed in life. The school systems appear to reward students for being cynical conformists who try to manipulate others through forced, fake behavior.[15] Although it is important to realize students enter college with this type of socialization, it is unclear how teachers can combat this mentality if higher education also rewards cynical conformity.

The authors of *Writing across Contexts* rightly argue that the role of grades in shaping high-school writers also affects the ability of students to take a more theoretical approach to their own compositions:

What this means, however, is that satisfying teacher expectations as the goal contributes to a fixed sense of writer identity: students see themselves dichotomously, as the good writers or bad writers they are now and will be forever. Moreover, the expectations themselves substitute for a more theoretical understanding of writing located in a concept like the rhetorical situation. In such cases, the concept

of the rhetorical situation has been distilled into a student-teacher
interaction. (Yancey, Robertson, and Taczak 2014, 108)

Grading and testing, then, can prevent transfer and metacognition because most learning situations are structured by the
role of the teacher in rewarding or punishing the student with
grades. It is therefore difficult to see how more effective teaching
and learning models can be implemented in higher education if
we do not act to change the ways we test and grade students on
all levels of education.

THE PROBLEM OF THE LITERARY

Another way politics enters the college writing classroom is that
most students in high school are mandated to be tested on literary texts in their English courses, but most of the writing they
must produce and consume in college is nonliterary:

> What this seems to mean for virtually all FYC students is that
> as students enter college writing classes, there's not only prior
> knowledge providing context, but also an absence of prior
> knowledge, and in two important areas: (1) key writing concepts
> and (2) non-fiction texts that serve as models. In part, such a situ-
> ation exists because the curricula at the two sites—high school
> and college—don't align well, a point underscored by propo-
> nents of the Common Core State Standards. In addition, as
> Applebee and Langer's (2011) continuing research on the high
> school English/language arts curriculum shows, the high school
> classroom is a literature classroom, whereas the first-year writ-
> ing classroom, which—despite the diverse forms it takes, from
> first-year seminars to WAC-based approaches to cultural studies
> and critical pedagogy approaches (see Fulkerson 2005; Harris
> 2006)—is typically a writing classroom. (Yancey, Robertson, and
> Taczak 2014, 108)

The focus on literature in high-school English classes then
shapes the expectations of student writers when they enter college, and these expectations affect their ability to learn new ways
of writing, thinking, and reading:

> Second is the way that writing is positioned in the high
> school classes Applebee and Langer (2011) studied: chiefly as

preparation for test-taking, with the single purpose of passing a
test, and the single audience of Britton et al.'s (1979) "teacher-
as-examiner." Moreover, this conclusion echoes the results of
the University of Washington Study of Undergraduate Learning
(SOUL) on incoming college writers (Beyer, Fisher, and Gilmore
2007), which was designed to identify the gaps between high
school and college that presented obstacles to students. Their
findings suggest that the major gaps are in math and writing,
and that writing tests themselves limit students' understanding
of and practice in writing. As a result, writing's purposes are
truncated and its potential to serve learning is undeveloped.
As Applebee and Langer (2011) remark, "Given the constraints
imposed by high-stakes tests, writing as a way to study, learn, and
go beyond—as a way to construct knowledge or generate new
networks of understandings . . . is rare" (26). The scholarship
on the transition from high school to college thus focuses on a
fundamental key concept: a definition and practice of writing for
authentic purposes and genuine audiences. (Yancey, Robertson,
and Taczak 2014, 109)

The problem with this formulation is that it implies that once
students get to college, they are finally able to write for real
audiences with real purposes, but the reality is that many noncomposition college classes do not provide opportunities to
write in a more critical, creative, or engaged fashion.

HOW TO TEACH FOR TRANSFER

At the end of their study, the authors of *Writing across Contexts*
outline the basic elements of their teaching-for-transfer (TFT)
approach.

Based on our TFT study, and the recommendations in *How
People Learn* (Bransford, Pellegrino, and Donovan 2000), we
can make six general suggestions for effective teaching for
transfer. 1. Be explicit. Writing is a social practice; it's governed
by conventions, so it changes over time. Writing requires both
practice and knowledge, which is what a FYC course provides.
These are very explicit lessons, and as the research on learning
demonstrates, if we want students to learn them we do better to
be straightforward in our teaching. 2. Build in expert practices.
Describing practices is helpful; demonstrating them is better,

in part because it shows what's expected, in part because it illustrates how what is expected can be accomplished. 3. Tap prior knowledge and concurrent knowledge. As explained in HPL and demonstrated by our students, prior knowledge is the base from which we all learn. Explaining what we think we know—moving from the tacit to the explicit—is a first step toward the remixing of prior knowledge engaged in by successful students. In addition, since students' learning isn't static, it's important to include learning that is occurring at the same time a student is in a given class. 4. Include processes and link them to key terms and a framework. The composition field, we think, takes considerable pride in its success improving teaching processes (although we share some of the reservations expressed by Matsuda [2003] and DeJoy [2004]), but processes, and they are plural, need to be connected to a framework located in key terms, in our case rhetorical situation, genre, discourse community, and so on. 5. Consistently ask students to create their own frameworks using prior knowledge. Learning doesn't occur in a linear way for most people; we tack, and reiterative assignments support such tacking by inviting students to revisit what they have learned in light of new information and experience. However, the learning also has to be mapped onto a larger framework lest it function as an intellectual GPS device. 6. Build in metacognition, verbal and visual, balancing big picture and small practices. The field has recognized the value of reflection for some time (Belanoff 2001; Yancey 1998, 2009b), though often it is focused exclusively on process. Given the success we see in supporting the transfer of process, there is every reason to expand our use of reflection, especially if it is integrated into conceptual center and assignment design, as we do in the TFT course. Despite these general maxims and our research telling us that teaching for transfer can be successful, our teaching experience with the TFT course also tells us that success doesn't come easily. (Yancey, Robertson, and Taczak 2014, 138–39)

Even though these moves to make the teaching of writing more explicit and theoretical should be lauded, one must wonder how writing studies can advance if it does not take on the educational structures that work against its efforts. Students don't just need a map to navigate their internal mental landscapes; they need a learning environment that is engaging and reflective.

At the end of their work, the authors do indeed tie the question of how to teach in an effective manner to the use of contingent faculty in composition courses:

> While we know the Teaching for Transfer course is successful in fostering transfer, and we are currently exploring how it can be successfully adapted to different contexts of teaching and learning, we also know its "delivery" might pose a challenge. A large percentage of those teaching FYC in this country are contingent faculty or teaching assistants without the training in rhetoric and composition that was advantageous for us in teaching the course successfully. How to provide sufficient information to enable these instructors to feel confident in teaching a TFT course is thus a key factor in helping students transfer knowledge and practice. We might begin with questions like the ones we share here, since we would then engage as teacher-researchers together. (Yancey, Robertson, and Taczak 2014, 147)

Perhaps the focus on metacognition and developing the right curriculum for transfer allows these writers to imagine that the material labor conditions facing composition can be overcome through intellectual activity, but history is against this spiritual transcendence of social relations.

NOTES

1.   To better understand how self-awareness can actually block political and social progress, one can look at the history of feminism as it is presented in Susan Douglas (2010).

2.   For the relation between grade obsession and high school, see Pope (2001).

3.   Perkins and Salomon (1992) help clarify the difference between easy and difficult forms of transferring knowledge from one context to the next.

4.   See Labaree (2012) for the concept of "doing school."

5.   As I will discuss in chapter 4, this theory of genre often leads to teaching students how to conform to any new social context, and in this way, it represents a neoliberal mode of subjectivity and ideology: since one cannot change society, all one can do is try to make it work for oneself in a cynical manner.

6.   For a critique of the use of large lecture classes, see Samuels (2013), 27–42.

7.   A dialogical approach to pedagogy is discussed in David Skidmore (2000).

8.   The theory of metacognition runs into several philosophical problems: (1) there are limits to self-knowledge; (2) many of our mental processes

work best by being unconscious or preconscious; and (3) self-awareness can bring mental paralysis

9.   This concept of cynical conformity is derived from Magill (2009), Peter Sloterdijk (1988), and Žižek (1989).

10.   See Samuels (2013, 4–5).

11.   For critiques of student evaluations, see Todd Riniolo et al. (2006), Stark and Freishtat (2014), and Paul Trout (1998).

12.   This relation between what students transfer and their psychological dispositions is discussed by Carl Bereiter (1995).

13.   See Adler-Kassner and O'Neill (2010).

14.   See Adler-Kassner and O'Neill (2010), Kohn (2000), and Samuels (2013).

15.   Cynical conformity in education is discussed at length by Pope (2001).

4

GENRE AS SOCIAL CONFORMITY
Charles Bazerman after Postmodernity

This analysis of Charles Bazerman's (2012) "Genre as Social Action" seeks to place the concept of genre in a social, intellectual, and political context. The overall argument is that genre is often presented as a recurrent, typical mode of social communication, and this theory tends to reinforce a discourse of social conformity. In terms of writing studies and the teaching of composition, we have seen how genre plays a central role in the argument that writing is always defined by specific contexts and for particular purposes, yet the theory of genre is itself a generalized approach to language, culture, and social interaction. While it may appear that teaching students how to adjust to specific genres is a progressive step beyond the notion that composition teaches only basic skills, my contention is that Bazerman's conception of genre reveals a more conservative aspect of this important concept.

HOW SOCIAL LANGUAGE WORKS

Bazerman begins his text by proposing a general definition of the way language functions in society: "Discourse arises among people in interaction and is part of the means by which people accomplish social actions. Meanings arise within the pragmatic unfolding of events and mediate the alignment of participants to perceptions of immediate situations and relevant contexts (whether fictive or non-fictive) called to mind by language" (218). The first move here is to establish language as a social and pragmatic tool that allows individuals to accomplish shared goals. Part of this process is identified as using both fictive and nonfictive contexts in order to mediate social interaction.[1] Yet,

DOI: 10.7330/9781607325840.c004

embedded in this argument is a very subtle assumption that social interactions are primarily mediated by meanings. In other words, to accomplish shared goals, individuals must use meanings in order to align their perceptions of a situation. In a move similar to Jürgen Habermas's theory of communicative rationality, Bazerman implies that a system of shared understanding regulates social action.[2] Moreover, his second assumption is that it may not matter whether the mediating meanings are real or fictional.

Following Carolyn Miller's (1984) important work "Genre as Social Action," Bazerman stresses that his theory of communication sees genre as a typified social convention, which is enacted by socially constructed individuals:

> Language is crafted, deployed, and interpreted by individuals in the course of social participation, even when individuals use language in a personally reflective mode, considering one's own identity, commitments, and actions using received language. Language users (with particular neurophysiological capacities and individual histories of language experience) in the course of interaction call upon the resources of language that are socially and culturally available and that have been typified through histories of social circulation; nonetheless, individuals construct meanings and consequentiality from their perception of particular novel situations and their participant action in those situations. (Bazerman 2012, 218)

The move here is not only to stress the social nature of both genres and individual reflections but to argue that these recurrent forms allow individuals to produce meanings that work with unique experiences. Like the combination of fiction and reality mentioned above, this combination of the typified and the unique serves to fuse conflicting categories and allows for a contradictory ideology in which the social and the individual are sewn together.[3] In fact, I argue that a key to understanding the current neoliberal ideology that shapes higher education and our political discourse revolves around the way we use language to combine opposing elements of material reality. From this perspective, the main function of contemporary ideology is to bypass real social conflicts by imagining on an intellectual level the seamless combination of opposites, like the combination of fact and fiction and self and other. Thus, instead of people acting to change material conflicts, they mentally conflate opposing forces.

To substantiate the larger claim I am making, we can return to the text and determine the underlying theory of language and society that supports Bazerman's articulation of genre. In discussing the role of meaning and social action in genre, he posits the following definition: "Thus situated meaning is a negotiation between the public distribution and practices of language expected within the site of communication and the personal meaning systems of the receiving individuals, developed through a lifetime of socially-embedded language use, as applied to the communicative issue at hand" (Bazerman 2012, 218). In this ideal state of social communication, socially influenced individuals negotiate meanings. Once again, this seemingly straightforward definition is packed with assumptions regarding language, society, subjectivity, and politics. First of all, the term *negotiation* signals a mode of communication in which there is a give and take between different social actors. This type of structure does not lend itself to representing non-recognition, misunderstanding, conflicting views, dissensus, or uncertainty.[4] Furthermore, the stress on individual meanings developed through socially embedded language returns to the nonproblematized social individual. We shall see that this view of human subjectivity appears to be centered on a model of social conformity and a neglect of the disruptive and disrupting aspects of communication.[5]

For Bazerman, genres promote social actions through cooperation: "We may use language both to cooperate in building a stone wall physically in front of us as well as to establish principles of chemical bonding in scientific publications (which, however, index and are accountable to the material chemical interactions in specialized experimental probes and in everyday life.) We may even use language to transport the imaginations of our audience into imagined events in a fictive galaxy where fundamental principles of the world we know are suspended"

(Bazerman 2012, 218). Here social cooperation is compared to a chemical process and a fictional world. In this rhetorical move, social constructions are naturalized and nature and society are associated with fictional worlds. The ideological work of this theory of genre, then, concerns the way the social status quo is rendered both natural and constructed.[6] In other words, the foundational oppositions of modern culture (truth versus fiction, social versus individual, culture versus nature) are overcome through a rhetoric of linguistic mediation.

Bazerman at times does look at moments in which the naturalized social world of mutual understanding is disrupted, but for the most part, his conception of genre depicts a friction-free world of reciprocal communication: "In investigating meaning making of cleverly creative people in variable circumstances (though not without constraints), we need to identify the processes by which language users create order and sense so as to align with each other for mutual understanding and coordination. These coordinations build on simple grounds but lead to the complexity of the discursive world as we know it" (Bazerman 2012, 218). Once again, the focus on coordination and cooperation pushes our understanding of genre in the direction of social conformity and consensus. In this structure, genres represent typical sets of expectations that reinforce a sense of mutual understanding even when people do not really comprehend each other.[7]

Bazerman indicates that writing often leads to misunderstanding, but he associates this lack of mutual comprehension to difficult or unfamiliar texts: "The problem of alignment over limited clues is most poignant when the text is written in a hard-to-read script or in a language the reader has limited familiarity with. Then the reader may be left with just inkmarks on paper that cannot be animated into meanings and intentions. Even if the reader is highly literate in the language, ambiguous words, unfamiliar references, novel ideas, difficult syntax, or complex arguments can make an act of reading an imaginative and interpretive challenge" (Bazerman 2012, 219). The goal here appears to be to use genre as way of overcoming difficult written texts, but we must examine the theory of communication undergirding this argument. For example, a difficult or hard-to-read text may challenge a reader to slow down and think more deeply about what is written. In fact, some studies have shown that a teacher who is very easy to understand may give the students the illusion of comprehension when they in reality learn very little; likewise, a difficult and disorganized teacher may force students to examine the class material in a more careful and critical manner.[8]

If learning often involves challenging previous beliefs or understandings, the emphasis on effortless communication may be misleading. To be clear, my argument is not that people should be intentionally dense or difficult; rather, we must resist equating clear writing with mutual understanding. Often, people exchange the same social symbols but understand those symbols in different ways. As Bazerman himself points out, "Even when only fully common words, genres and constructions are used, the different associations, cognitive patterns, and interests of different readers can make reanimating another's meanings a challenge with only approximate results—otherwise there would be no fields of hermeneutics, literary criticism, legal disputation, and scriptural interpretation. . . . Nor would reader response need theorizing" (Bazerman 2012, 219). This failure of people to share the same meanings threatens to undermine Bazerman's theory of genre, yet he finds many different ways to make this deconstructive problem go away.[9]

DISRUPTING DISRUPTION

One way the disruptive aspects of language are contained is through an understanding of genre as a metacognitive social activity:

> The answer proposed in this chapter and the kinds of work reported here is that the problem of recognizability of meaning is in large part a matter of recognizing situations and actions within which the meanings are mobilized through the medium of the signs. Meaning is not fully available and immanent in

the bare spelled words. Interactants' familiarity with domains of communication and relevant genres make the kind of communication recognizable: establishing roles, values, domains of content, and general actions which then create the space for more specific, detailed refined utterances and meanings spelled out in the crafted words. (Bazerman 2012, 219)

Mutual understanding is thus saved by basing communication on established social roles, values, and generalized actions. In other terms, deconstruction and misunderstanding are replaced by social conformity and a reflective knowledge about how language functions in particular contexts.

This model of communication makes it hard to understand how learning and social change can ever happen. If people return to established roles and values in order to escape from the pitfalls of linguistic confusion, genre devalues new knowledge, new values, and changing social positions. Of course, Bazerman is aware of this attempt to control language through nondiscursive means, but once the genie of disruption appears, it must be constantly stuffed back into the bottle. Thus, in his discussion of interpersonal communication, he imports a moral vocabulary to reregulate the need for mutual understanding:

Attentiveness to the words, choosing the right words, and being loyal to the words written by others supports the hard work of writing intelligibly and intelligently to readers and of sympathetically reconstructing the meanings other writers attempt to evoke. Attention to the details of each other's expressions is part of an ethics of interpersonal, social engagement. However, practical attention to language always occurs within situations that orient the participants and evoke particular expectations and knowledge worlds, even if only tacitly and habitually. (Bazerman 2012, 220)

Two different rhetorical strategies help structure this passage: on the one hand, a language of ethics and loyalty is used to impose a moral order, and on the other hand, a discourse of pragmatism and temporality is employed to allow for the seamless fusion of generalization and uniqueness. Therefore, genre can only function to ensure communication by reaching outside and making a moral claim as it combines loyalty with pragmatism.[10]

The pragmatic moralist can be considered to be a model of subjectivity required by genre: one must adjust to new situations by remaining faithful to preestablished social hierarchies. In what we can call the *neoliberal consensus,* conservative and liberal notions of communication and social order have merged so people learn how to conform to an ever-changing world. Bazerman highlights this new subjectivity in the following discussion of using genre in a writing class:

> Aiding student development to read and write in situations with which they are less familiar (such as those in research disciplines or professions) requires we become explicit about the communicative situations, social organization, and activities they are engaging. Making explicit the organization and dynamics of communicative situations helps students know more concretely what their options are and how they might frame their goals, enhancing the potential for communicative success. The articulation of goals and repeated success in achieving them feeds back into increased motivation and engagement. (Bazerman 2012, 220)

Underlying this seemingly benign call for increasing students' knowledge of communicative situations, we find the assumption that the goal of education is to help students understand and then master particular social contexts. There does not seem to be much space here for critiquing or changing the social structure; rather, the impulse is for social conformity through individual awareness.

Unlike many of the poststructuralist and postmodern theorists, who had a much more abstract and systemic understanding of how language works, Bazerman returns to genre and pragmatism as stabilizing local structures:

> While linguistics has done well in creating abstracted accounts of language based on the regularized practices of groups of language users, we must take seriously that these are only transient formations, constantly evolving, various in their local instantiations and used creatively and purposefully by each user in a specific set of circumstances. Accordingly words are effective within the situation but do not have a timeless meaning in themselves. They serve as clues within a situation to align participants and

achieve local actions. This view is consistent with theories of reading that suggest we make hypotheses about the meaning of texts based on our previous knowledge and experience, the encounter with the text prior to the current moment, and our continuing monitoring in further reading for contradictory evidence which might reassert meaning as an unsolved puzzle. (Bazerman 2012, 220)

This pragmatic emphasis on using typical structures in specific, local contexts works against the structuralist and poststructuralist move to see language as an autonomous social system.[11] Although there are important benefits concerning the use of genre to focus on specific and particular social contexts, there is a risk that a pragmatic turn undermines our ability to document the ways language and communication sometimes fail. Moreover, without a more structural approach, it is hard to develop a coherent understanding of the multiple levels of language and discourse.[12]

When Bazerman does look at language problems, he often examines isolated conflicts and not systemic issues:

The complexity of meaning making is visible when we see how fragmentary and indefinite utterances of young children are interpreted proleptically by the care givers around (Cole 1996; van Lier 2004), how people negotiate meanings and activities in high noise environments, or in the constant need for repair in spoken language as investigated by conversational analysts (Sacks 1995; Schegloff, Sacks and Jefferson 1977). The attempts at utterances are taken as completed when the parties decide that their needs/actions are met well enough or when they give up the endeavor or accept lower degrees of approximation, good enough for all practical purposes, as phrased in phenomenology (Schutz 1967; Schutz & Luckmann 1973) and ethnomethodology (Garfinkel 1967). (Bazerman 2012, 220)

This pragmatic understanding of language steers a middle ground between the postmodern deconstructive position that language always misses or displaces its referent and the modern notion of language as a transparent medium. However, this post-postmodern happy medium may rely on replacing social antagonism with social conformity.

In a culture that has commodified diversity and dissent, the conflict between the individual and the social is often transcended by the imaginary (con)fusion of the self and the Other.[13] With genre, typical social situations are interpreted by socially constructed individuals in specific social contexts, and in this combination of the social and the individual, success is defined by social conformity. For example, in Bazerman's celebration of successful alignments of meaning, the problematic aspects of communication are highlighted in order to applaud an ideal order of social agreement: "All language is an approximate indicator of meaning, with some situations having narrower tolerances for accuracy and alignment than others. Rather than taking transparency of language as the norm, we rather should take those situations that achieve high degrees of alignment, shared meaning, and reliability of co-reference as specific accomplishments, to be examined for the special means of achievement in their situation" (Bazerman 2012, 221). Here, the ability of people to share meanings and to cooperate is seen as a special situation worthy of praise and deep respect, and while I would not want to undermine the value of cooperation in certain situations, the privileging of mutuality tends to devalue critique, dissensus, confrontation, innovation, and transformation.[14] Furthermore, linguistic cooperation may represent a false theory of how language and social interaction actually function.

THE MYTH OF MIRROR NEURONS

To better understand Bazerman's underlying theory of language and subjectivity, we can look at how he employs genre to define social communication:

> Available and familiar patterns of utterances (that is, genres) provide interpretable clues that allow people to make sense of each other's utterances and to frame utterances meaningful to one's interlocutors (Bazerman 2003). Mead (1934) has in fact proposed that our sense of the self arises from our attempts to represent our meanings to be intelligible to others within a social

field. The recent discovery of mirror neurons may provide neurological basis for the abilities to take the part of the other and to
reconstruct what another's meaning might have been (Rizzolatti
& Criaghero 2004). From a Vygotskian perspective we may say
that the internalized words provide the means of regulating our
cognitive and affective states as we orient towards social interaction (Vygotsky 1987). Whatever the developmental, cognitive
and neurological processes in aligning to social symbols, genre
identifies the recognizable kind of utterance we believe we are
producing or receiving. (Bazerman 2012, 221)

The chain of evidence here is the following: (1) familiar patterns of communication (genres) allow people to make sense
of each other's utterances; (2) George Herbert Mead argued
that our sense of self is derived from our attempts at communication; (3) mirror neurons may prove we can mentally inhabit
the mind of others; and (4) internalized discourses help us
regulate our own thoughts and feelings for social purposes.
I contend that all of these processes revolve around organizing our inner mental processes for the purpose of social conformity: we use genres in order to standardize our thoughts
and words so we can imagine what other people are thinking,
and this mind reading enables us to not only understand others, but also to shape our own thoughts and feelings to match
the thoughts and feelings of others. What is problematic then
about this theory of empathic social understanding is that (1)
mirror neurons are imaginary scientific constructions created
in order to substantiate the theory of empathy; (2) the theory
of empathy is evoked in order to create the illusion that people
can really fully understand and experience the same thing others are experiencing; and (3) we want to believe in the same-
ness of our mental experiences in order to enhance the illusion
of social cohesion.[15]

   In contrast to the theory of empathic communication, psychoanalysis and experience tell us no one can fully access another
person's consciousness, and the illusion of mutual understanding can result in a condescending and patronizing attitude.
Moreover, one of the things that makes us human is that we
do have mental freedom, which leads to creativity, innovation,

revolution, personality, and a quest for uniqueness. Paradoxically, this freedom of the individual is often based on the fact that many of our actions are not the result of conscious intention; instead, the theories of the unconscious and social determinism tell us we often act in an automatic and intuitive way.

Both psychoanalysis and neuroscience have documented the problems with basing communication and social action on the intentionality of the individual, but Bazerman's theory is indicative of the tendency in writing studies to ignore this critique of intentionality.[16] For instance, the following passage bases communication on intention:

> Within the actual contexts of use, utterances are the minimal unit, aimed at influencing others as part of our cooperative and competitive social interactions, minimally understandable as an act, an intention, a meaning to be transmitted. Its recognizability makes it perceivable as an intended act, an intended influence, an intended transformation of the interlocutor's attention and orientation. In a fundamental way, an utterance acts as the utterer's attempt to define the situation as a site of action for his or her utterance, what in rhetoric would be called the rhetorical situation (Bitzer 1968) or *kairos* (Miller 1992) and what Goffman might consider as footing or framing (Goffman 1974, 1981). Miller (1984), following Schutz's concept of typification (1967), has associated genre with a typified response to a typified situation. That is, the utterer sees the moment as similar to other moments in which certain kinds of utterances have been effective. Insofar as these typifications and their attendant instantiating moments are circulated and familiar within the group of interlocutors, they facilitate mutual comprehension and intelligibility of an utterance within a shared recognized context (Bazerman 1994b). (Bazerman 2012, 221)

I read this passage as an attempt to move beyond the problems brought up by psychoanalysis, deconstruction, and neuroscience regarding the limits of intentionality and the roles played by the unconscious, irrationality, and dissensus. Thus, a more complex and realistic understanding of communication problematizes the writing studies concept of genre.

For Bazerman, genres are inherently conservative structures because they rely on typical social situations:

> An utterance noted and attended to is a speech act. What kind of
> speech act it is perceived as and what are the felicity conditions it
> must meet for success, are very much a matter of typification, in
> terms of how the interlocutor sees the situation and the utterance
> as an intervention in the situation. We judge what is happening
> now on the basis of what has come before—what has been under-
> stood, what has been the consequence, how events have typically
> unfolded, what has seemed an adequate understanding of the
> utterance acceptable by relevant parties. (Bazerman 2012, 222)

In terms of education, this stress on the successful use of typified genres feeds into the logic of cynical conformity in the
sense that students are trained to conform to the expectations
of their teachers in order to receive an external reward regardless of the students' own desires, beliefs, feelings, and values.
Thus, genre here is not being presented simply as a possible
tool for learning; rather, genre represents a strategy for social
success through (cynical) conformity:

> The successful speech act creates a social fact, both in the recog-
> nition of its accomplishment (e.g., we all agree you have made
> a bet, committed to a valid contract, etc.) and in terms of the
> contents represented and relied on (e.g., a sports event is going
> to occur at a certain time and venue with certain participants,
> upon which the bet is placed). Social facts are those things that
> people believe and are true in their consequences, whatever
> their accountable relation to material events may be. In fact
> strong social facts that run up against an accountable contradic-
> tion with material events create their own set of consequences—
> perhaps a riot at the sports venue when the gates are locked and
> the teams do not show, despite the contract on the printed ticket.
> (Bazerman 2012, 223)

Genres therefore shape speech acts, which create social facts
people believe even if they are in conflict with material reality.
Although Bazerman does posit that if the social facts contradict
material events, negative consequences may result, the emphasis is on the creation of a stable mental reality. Once again, there
is nothing wrong with thinking about communication in terms
of successful interactions, but problems arise when language
use is configured to rely on social conformity regardless of the
relation between language and reality.[17]

Bazerman's focus on the success of using typified genres and speech acts tends to create an idealized version of communication, society, education, and politics in which conformity triumphs over innovation, critique, conflict, difference, and unconscious irrationality. For instance, in the following passage, we return to the role played by typification in genre:

> Since utterances are the site for the creation and transmission of speech acts and social facts, the typification of utterances in genres is related to the recognizability of acts and the location of facts. Inversely, we can understand the effectiveness of texts in large part through their success in accomplishing speech acts and establishing social facts. Thus a successful bet or a successful court sentence or a successful scientific paper relies both on being enacted by the right participants in the appropriate situation, and on adopting a suitable form and meeting a series of expectations about the fact and reasoning presented within. In these different genred utterances and associated acts, there are particulars presented and reasoned about that also are accountable to other non-textual dimensions of the ambient worlds. These accountable relations are also structured through typified, genred understanding. Thus a court decision must appropriately index relevant laws, judicial rules, and precedents in such a way as to persuasively identify them as authoritative in this case; the decision as well hangs on appropriate indexing and consideration of the evidence. Somewhat differently, the scientific paper must articulate with prior theory and findings as aggregated in the relevant literatures (relevancy here also being a negotiated construction), as well as current evidence gathered in ways that meet evaluative criteria and expectations of the most influential peer readers. All these conditions must continue to stand for the text to be meaningful and consequential for the ongoing work of the court or scientific discipline. (Bazerman 2012, 223)

According to this theory, science and law function when the right people recognize typified genres in the proper context. In other words, an idealized conception of communication serves to rationalize and reinforce social discourses, and part of this idealization relies on the right people using the right words at the right moment. This underlying theory of communication forces the theory of genre to be centered on conforming to a meritocratic system of preestablished correctness: "Thus different genres are the origin, part of the validation system, and means of circulation, storage, and access of particular pieces of knowledge" (Bazerman 2012, 223). Here the validation of typified structures is shaped by the ability of genres to motivate communicators to conform to the expectation of accepted authorities.

My argument here is not that we should simply reject all conformity to typical representations, but we must question whether we want the teaching of writing to be focused on a discourse of normative assimilation. Yes, we can try to teach students to detect the conventions and constraints of particular genres, but do we want the goal of a writing class to be motivating students to conform to the surrounding social and educational structures? Also, is it possible to imagine a theory of genre not focused on conformity to typified structures? In short, what theory of genre would help us encourage students to be creative and critical? Moreover, how can we teach any critical theory of composition if students are locked into a testing and grading system that rewards conformity to the typified expectations of teachers?

THE POLITICS OF GENRE

As Bazerman indicates, the stakes for his theory of genre are high because they apply to the foundations of our political and social systems. For example, in the following example, he relates genre to the process of identifying someone's citizenship:

> This linkage between genres, speech acts, and social facts is visible when we, for example, seek to identify someone's citizenship. We know there are certain documentary locations where such information is established and kept, such as governmental records offices where birth certificates are filed or passport records are kept. Further, the documents in question not only store the information but in fact establish the legitimacy and facticity of the information, entering it into a network of related documents that refer and respond to each other. The intertextual link with the originary record maintains the legitimacy of all the secondary documents. Genres are typified not only in the facts they use, but in the other genres they typically draw on, refer to, or otherwise use. (Bazerman 2012, 224)

Here genre is given a social and even policing function, as specific texts are used to determine the status of a person's citizenship. As a web of interlocking texts, the network of typified social documents serves to control and regulate the populace.

It is interesting that Bazerman turns to the instance of using documents to establish citizenship as a key example of the way genres function in the real world. In reaching outside the composition classroom, he reveals that the use of texts within education are linked to our conceptions of writing in a broader social and political context. Policing the boundaries of genres can thus be seen as a political act dedicated to enforcing social control through the rewarding of social conformity. In fact, Bazerman constantly returns to notions of typification and regularization in order to define how genres are always placed in larger social networks:

> The systematic circulation of genres among particular groupings serves to mediate communications within an activity system, that is, a group of people in systematic relations in pursuit of work or transformations of the environment (Bazerman 1994a). The texts within these groups mediate communications (along with communications in other channels). The typification of message occasions and structures social and organizational relations in pursuit of the system's ends, providing a regularized communicative infrastructure. Within the genres of activity systems, the typified epistemic and ontological choices as well as typical concepts, roles, stances, evaluations, lexicon, intertextuality, and other linguistic features serve in effect something like Foucault's (1970) episteme or discourse, inscribing an ideology and defining power relations. (Bazerman 2012, 224)

This description of the power relations shaping the use of genres comes off as being neutral and objective, yet buried in this discourse is a set of assumptions concerning how language is centered on social control, repetition, prediction, and normalization.

In contrast to Bazerman's conception of genre, we can look at Bill Readings's (1996) *The University in Ruins*, in which he makes a strong call to resist the pressure for communication, unity, and consensus in higher education; instead, Readings promotes the role of dissensus, complexity, and difference in learning and social discourse. From Readings's perspective, teaching should be about opening up a space for dialogues, debate, and distinct views and not about conforming to the discourse of the instructor. If we apply this argument to Bazerman's sense of genre and social discourse, we must ask how we can provide a theory of language that opens up discussion and does not call for conformity. Furthermore, instead of seeing language as creating shared meanings, how do we envision discourse and writing as the exploration of differences?

TURNING ON THE LIGHT

Returning to Bazerman's text, his long discussion of Edison's use of genres is instructive because it is centered on a discourse of combining science and business in a successful manner:

> Edison, for example, understood better than his competitors that the project of developing a system of electric light and power required the enlistment of many groups of people. Edison needed to create presence, meaning, and value for electric light and power within their respective discursive systems. His prior experience as a childhood newsboy, as a freelance electrical inventor, as a patent holder, as a contractor to telephone and telegraph industrialists, and as a news celebrity following the invention of the phonograph prepared him to translate the meanings of his proposed project to seek support. (Bazerman 2012, 225)

Edison is celebrated here for his great ability at marketing his scientific discoveries, but from Readings's perspective, it is precisely this combination of science and capitalism that undermines the ability of universities to offer a space for free debate and discovery. Instead of insisting on the modern separation of science as the pure pursuit of truth and capitalism as rational self-interest, Bazerman's discourse here calls for a suturing of the modern divide.[18]

Edison's understanding of distinct genres and discourses is presented as a model for how students must learn to integrate different discourse communities in their writing, yet Bazerman himself highlights the way Edison used his celebrity to manipulate his audiences:

> Understanding how telegraphy, railroad distribution, and urban-
> ization were creating a new kind of public forum, he saw the
> importance celebrity interviews and feature stories were taking
> to sell newspapers; he soon learned to become a good interview
> subject in order to publicize his new ventures. Understanding
> the rise of new financial markets to support large enterprises
> based on new technology, he was able to present his project as a
> potential financial bonanza to a cadre of elite investors and then
> later to financial markets. Understanding the patent system and
> the complexity of patent litigation, he and his attorneys were able
> to create a web of protections that maintained his ownership of a
> rapidly changing technology. Understanding how to draw on the
> skills of his inventive collaborators and communicate effectively
> with them, he was able to invent a new kind of industrial labora-
> tory coordinated through a set of shared laboratory notebooks
> and other documents. (Bazerman 2012, 225)

Genre as a form of rhetorical persuasion is positioned here as
akin to advertising and self-promotion, and in this social discourse, there is little space for a notion of writing outside com-
merce, conformity, and consensus. We see here how the neoliberal push to redefine education as preparation for capitalist
exploitation emerges in a seemingly benign description of how
genre functions.

Bazerman's turn to Edison is interesting because he also
reveals that this inventor's success was in part derived from a set
of unethical activities:

> With the help of his colleagues he understood the importance
> of representing the electric light as an attractive enhancement
> to new forms of urban domesticity. His energetic representations
> of the light in each of these forums were fundamental to his
> success. These representations were so important to him that he
> was willing to adopt unconventional means to make sure that he
> got the representations he needed, including bribing journalists,
> paying off city officials, packing scientific juries, and giving inside
> information to investors. The one major communicative failure,
> in turning the charismatic personal communications of his early
> companies into more regularized bureaucratic communications
> of a large corporation, contributed to his loss of ownership of
> General Edison, which became General Electric (Bazerman
> 1999a). (Bazerman 2012, 225)

Edison is indeed a strange model for students to follow in learning about how to use genres in an effective manner. Once again, Bazerman presents this example in a neutral, value-free way, but his reluctance to question Edison's unethical behavior can function to normalize a manipulative and antisocial view of language use.

Embedded in Bazerman's neutral description of genre use, we have found a set of ideological assumptions that must be unpacked. While it is tempting to imagine writing studies as an academic discourse void of political ramifications, we have seen that descriptions of language usage are rarely nonideological; in fact, the desire to create a neutral, nonideological space is one of the major ideological moves of the current period.

Due to the ever-increasing amounts of information that confront us daily, we often try to find a way to control the discourses around us, and genres have been shown to offer an effective way to translate social discourse into typical forms and predictable patterns. The question remains whether this use of genres to control information also functions to control individuals and institute a culture of cynical conformity. My reading of Bazerman's theory detects an underlying discourse of social conformity and social control through language typification. The question remains of how we should approach this type of discourse inside and outside the composition classroom.

NOTES

1. One of the underlying themes of this chapter is that the post-postmodern conception of the social is tied to an uncritical notion of multicultural pluralism. Like Hal Foster's (1985) critique of contemporary art, I am arguing that by embracing any and all cultures and discourses, one is merely refusing to make choices and judgments. In this structure, social conformity emerges as a dominant subjectivity because people are socialized to adjust to any new social situation.

2. For a critique of Habermas's theory, see Tewdwr-Jones and Allmendinger (1998).

3. One of the central arguments of this book is that current neoliberal ideology must convince people that they freely choose their social alienation; thus, conformity and freedom must be combined through a contradictory rhetoric.

4. For the need to base education and culture on dissensus, see Readings (1996).

5. We can read Bazerman's theory as a backlash against deconstruction and the postmodern troubling of linguistic transparency and clarity.

6. One reoccurring theme in neoliberal discourse is the naturalization of social hierarchies. We find this ideology deconstructed in Lewontin, Rose, and Kamin (1984).

7. Throughout his work, Lacan (1998) argues against the illusions of understanding and communications. Instead of seeing the analyst as the one who is supposed to know the truth, Lacan argues that analytic interpretation must disrupt the imaginary anticipation of shared meanings. One of the reasons for the critique is the idea that due to the autonomy of language in the unconscious, people do not even understand their own thoughts, let alone the thoughts of others.

8. For examples of how difficult and unclear texts and discourse can lead to better understanding and attention, see Trout (1998).

9. Throughout this text, I have been arguing that the current use of genre in writing studies often results in a dismissal of deconstruction and postmodernism, a move that plays into the neoliberal ideology of social conformity.

10. The strategy of my reading here follows Derrida's methodology of locating an unmarked political factor in rhetorical moves. Thus, as language tries to account for itself, it must constantly turn to external social and personal aspects to contain any disruption.

11. I am referring primarily to the works of Lacan (1998) and Derrida (1978) when I discuss the poststructuralist theories of language.

12. Lacan (1998) argues that if we really understood each other through language, there would be no need for interpretation or questioning.

13. For more on the commodification of dissent see Naomi Klein (1999).

14. One of the noticeable problems of the contemporary college classroom is that students are often uncomfortable discussing any issues that cause conflict or tension. In fact, we can see new media as feeding the desire of people to only interact with others who share the same views and values (see Pariser 2011).

15. For a deconstruction of the science of mirror neurons, see Gregory Hickok (2014). The current obsession with empathy in education circles is critiqued by Paul Bloom (2014).

16. For a discussion of the ways psychoanalysis and neuroscience challenge the notion of intentionality, see Antonio Damasio (2008) and Daniel Kahneman (2011).

17. Central to Lacan's entire critique of language and communication is the idea that the real can never be fully grasped by language, so we obsessively try to force reality to conform to social formations through language use.

18. My critique of this combination of science and capitalism is echoed in Kirp (2009), Christopher Newfield (2008), and Washburn (2008).

5
WRITING THEORY, IGNORING LABOR
Sid Dobrin and the Posthuman Subject

Throughout this book, we have witnessed an attempt of writing studies specialists to establish this new field as a research discipline in order to gain resources and respect. This institutional strategy usually relies on using the concepts of genre, transfer, and metacognition to study how students actually learn and apply new knowledge, and by combining research with teaching, the field is positioned to overcome the standard hierarchy structuring contemporary universities. I have stressed that the central problem in this institutional strategy is that due to its inability to transform larger social and educational structures, there is a tendency to promote a discourse of social conformity.

We shall see that in the case of Sid Dobrin's *Postcomposition*, the strategy is to fully identify with the dominant university research paradigm by privileging theory over teaching and by discrediting the current endeavor to focus on teaching students how to improve their writing in first-year composition courses. Like many other writing studies specialists, Dobrin (2011) believes the only way writing instruction can escape from its oppressive administrative function is for the field to abandon modern conceptions of subjectivity, writing, teaching, and discourse. He therefore turns to theory in order to break the connection between writing and composition: "This book, *Postcomposition*, underscores these differences, identifying composition (studies) as an academic discipline and composing as an act that is chained by that discipline to an understanding of student subjects performing that act (often only as academic performance). Writing is a phenomenon that requires the attention of intellectual and scholarly inquiry and speculation

DOI: 10.7330/9781607325840.c005

beyond composition. Writing is more than composition (studies)" (Dobrin 2011, 2). The main move Dobrin wants to make in order to free writing from its connection to teaching students how to compose is to expand our notion of what writing is today. Instead of seeing writing studies as centered on researching how to help students write in an effective manner, he aims to make a break with all practical and pragmatic considerations.[1]

One reason Dobrin urges us to move away from a focus on the practice of teaching writing is that he sees this project as representing a collusion with administrative control: "Embedded within that imperative is a need to call to question composition studies' conservative allegiance to subject and administration and the strictures that such allegiances have imposed on the field" (3). From a certain perspective, it would be hard to deny that teachers of writing must conform to administrative priorities and that the these priorities often are centered on teaching first-year composition, but the question remains, how can these institutional structures be challenged?

Instead of calling for collective action to transform universities and make them more responsive to students and the faculty, Dobrin asks for a theoretical reconceptualization:

> Simply put, what I argue for in these pages is that composition studies requires (or perhaps is already witnessing) a shift from the disciplinary focus upon (writing) subjects and pedagogy to a more explicit focus on writing itself. The danger for composition studies in the argument I unfold here is that it removes the ethical guarantor, the safety net, to what the discipline does. Without the solidity of student subjects and administration, of seeing this as a teaching field, there is no certainty for the field; the posts have been taken down. In order for composition studies to adhere to its mythologies, there must be a guarantor, but, a la Slavoj Zizek, we must know there never is a guarantor. The guarantor is merely a deferred position. For composition studies not to have a tangible guarantor is a frightening contingency, but contingencies are precisely the possibilities of writing. (Dobrin 2011, 3)

On one level, he is arguing that composition has been playing it safe by defining itself by its pragmatic role in teaching undergraduate students how to write; however, on a deeper level, he is also redefining writing itself as contingency.

Of course the turn toward contingency can seem ironic in a field plagued by contingent labor, but Dobrin shows little interest in this issue. What he does tend to focus on is the way teachers of writing are forced to monitor and discipline their students: "That is to say, composition studies' primary object of study is not writing or even the teaching of writing, as the field often claims; the field's primary object of study is the (student) subject" (Dobrin 2011, 4). Once again, there is a certain truth to this claim since the field does pay a lot of attention to how students, think, write, and read, and this focus may not be a bad thing in itself, but Dobrin wants us to make a radical step and imagine composition without subjects: "In order to initiate moves beyond the limits of the discipline, I take an approach that blends disciplinary critique with an attempt to unfold (the beginning of) an ecological/networked theory of writing that does not rely upon subjects as a principle tenet of the theory"(4). Thus, in his turn to new media networks and complexity theory, Dobrin imagines a world where individual subjects no longer play a central role. However, he is not calling for a more social or collective type of consciousness; instead, he wants us to see subjects and writing as dispersed in networks.[2]

For Dobrin, the focus on students in composition requires an emphasis on individual subjects, which also implies administrative control and disciplinary coherence: "I consider the (e)state of composition studies, examining particularly the central importance of subjects and program administration to the missions of the field. Likewise, I regard the ways in which the disciplinary nuzzling up to subjectivity and administration has fostered an anti-theoretical climate within the field and has influenced the overall direction of what can be considered legitimate research within the field" (4). In his attempt here to privilege theory over practice, Dobrin claims that composition's relation to teaching students and administration undermines its ability to embrace high theory and an expanded notion of writing.

Part of this move to theoretical speculation requires shedding any connection to institutional structures and traditional professional associations:

> My objection to subject/subjectivity as fundamental to writing studies in mind, the fourth chapter levels a critique against the ever-growing importance of writing program administration to composition studies' identity. This critique addresses the very idea of administration as well as the professional organization of the Council of Writing Program Administrators. To move postcomposition requires that administration be abandoned as a useful part of the field. (Dobrin 2011, 4)

This radical call for the removal of administration appears to be a purely theoretical move because he does not offer any concrete replacement; in fact, this move can be seen as the classic academic strategy of denying material structures by focusing on purely speculative pronouncements.[3] Furthermore, Dobrin comes off as quite dismissive of the relation between composition and labor exploitation:

> A substantial amount of the field's "research" has been geared toward understanding why (and how) it became an academic discipline. That same research often embraces a narrative of oppression that empowers the field's self-sustained image, as Susan Miller has put it, as "the sad women in the basement" (Textual Carnivals 121). Much of the field's self-reflective narrative has focused on validation of the work that it does. But, much of the work that examines composition studies' history and its evolution into an academic field presents that evolution as a primarily epistemological endeavor, as a development of intellectual and pedagogical need. Rarely do such historical assessments account for a bureaucratic history, beyond, perhaps, narratives of how writing instructors were and are treated as labor and devalued in relation to those who taught literature. Those conversations, however, are usually cast in terms of the power struggle between rhetoric and literature; that is, those conversations, despite their evidence of labor issues, are presented as representative of larger epistemological power struggles. (Dobrin 2011, 5)

It is hard to tell whether Dobrin is simply blaming the victim and rejecting the need for the field to pay attention to the use and abuse of contingent labor, but what is clear is that every time he approaches the issue of material relations, he runs toward speculative theorizations.[4]

Just as research universities often privilege theory over practice and reading and research over teaching, Dobrin tends to replicate the most oppressive hierarchies shaping academic institutions. Perhaps his idea is that if composition becomes another theory-driven discipline, it will gain respect and support. If this is the case, then his radical proposals and critiques are actually conservative endorsements of the status quo. Yet, it may be more effective to see his work as supporting a contradictory position that combines radical theory with a deep investment in the fundamental structures of the elite American research university. The ambiguity of his position can be detected in the following critique of the history of composition:

> In order for composition studies to become an academic field, those doing the work of composition studies had to persuade administrators that the teaching of rhetoric and writing was important enough to secure funding. With this funding (minimal as it may have been, at times) came efforts to ensure tenure lines in the field and provisions for developing a labor class within the field, as well. From these positions, then, composition studies could justify funding for journals, professional organizations, graduate programs, and all of the trappings that make and validate a discipline as disciplinary to its members and others in the academy. This bureaucracy, like any other, then, attains a state of self-perpetuation by creating its own audiences and need for publication and conferences as well as a system of self-replenishment through PhD programs in which the field replicates itself through disciplinary standards, core knowledge, and professional doctrine and lore. Pedagogy and epistemology do not exist outside of corporate/bureaucratic systems; to evaluate either without the other is to ignore a primary context of the other. In many ways, we might think of the division of epistemology and bureaucracy as a division between the philosophical and the political. (Dobrin 2011, 7)

On the one hand, this interpretation reads like a critique of the material history of the field of composition and the more general way academic research disciplines are established and maintained; but on the other hand, his desire for composition to attach itself to high theory reveals a commitment to the academic structures he is critiquing. While he examines the political economy of teaching, he does not appear to want to examine theory in the same critical light.

What I think Dobrin is arguing is that composition can only become a serious discipline if it becomes theoretical and gives up its ties to teaching, students, subjects, administrators, and labor issues:

> North nonetheless argues that "practical knowledge, the stuff of teachers' rooms, how-to articles, textbooks, and the like, doesn't count as research" (17). If composition studies cannot develop a coherent research agenda, North warns, then composition studies itself is "in serious trouble indeed" (17). North goes on to proclaim a new era of research, an era in which "the dominance of practice and sloppy research would have to end" (17). Unfortunately, the new era for which North called has not been achieved. (Dobrin 2011, 8)

Dobrin thus buys into the academic hierarchies that place research over teaching and theory over practice. Instead of arguing for the valuing of research on teaching and student learning, he wants the field to move in a more theoretical and speculative direction: "The past twenty-four years of scholarship in composition studies has largely served to institutionalize the inflated claims that classroom-based research counts as the primary form of disciplinary knowledge and to marginalize theory except as a way to explain or support what happens in the classroom" (8). As I have been arguing, Dobrin's privileging of pure theory over research on student learning feeds into many of the oppressive hierarchies shaping contemporary research universities, and his seemingly radical stance is in reality not only aligned with the dominant paradigm but also follows many of the recent claims for writing studies to act more like other respected disciplines.

Part of Dobrin's strategy to promote theory over classroom practices revolves around his setting up an opposition between exposing oppressive academic hierarchies and pure theory in composition research:

> In fact, composition studies has masterfully exploited its femi-
> nized and "othered" place in the academy to expose the biases
> of traditional forms of research, to draw attention to the pos-
> sible disciplinary value of teacher-based knowledge, and to make
> anecdote and narrative accepted forms of presentation for some
> scholarship. However, work to engage in research that does not
> rely upon or even mention classroom practice or application as
> either a source of or a goal of theory has often run up against
> resistance with a missionary zeal to minimize "theory for theory's
> sake." Composition studies casts the classroom and the class-
> room compositionists as heroic figures and construes research
> as useful only if it reports on or has application to classroom
> practice. (Dobrin 2011, 9)

Once again, it is hard to tell whether he is simply dismissing a
focus on teaching, students, and labor exploitation or arguing
that the field's focus on these material foundations has crowded
out a space for pure theory.

Although it is not always clear what Dobrin intends, he does
have a habit of mocking the financial and institutional considerations shaping the ways programs are funded and supported:
"And while Smit argues that composition studies must spread its
knowledge of writing instruction beyond the composition classroom, this move is little more than an attempt to create larger
populations of composition students in order to enlarge and
to further justify composition studies' territorial hold over 'student'" (Dobrin 2011, 10). In this cynical reading of the desire
to spread the importance of writing and writing instruction to
other fields and disciplines, Dobrin posits that David Smit's
(2004) focus on genre and transfer is really just a ploy to get
more students to take writing courses.[5]

Dobrin not only feels writing studies is seeking to cash in
by teaching more students, but he argues that the whole composition research process is centered on faking improvement,
gaining external validation, and finding an easy way to get published: "Composition studies' allegiance to research methodologies grounded in the classroom and the experiential/anec-
dotal have maintained such a strong foothold for three primary
reasons: simulacra improvement, institutional validation, and

ease. Composition studies has always proclaimed that it works to improve student writing, to make students better writers" (Dobrin 2011, 12). Therefore, at the same time Dobrin dismisses the material conditions of writing programs and composition faculty, he questions the true intentions of much of its research. We refind here the familiar trope of composition theorists undermining the value of the very field they inhabit. In an act of institutional suicide, all motives behind composition teaching and research are rendered suspect: "Composition studies, then, stands as a purveyor of betterment and enhancement. However, such improvement is false, a simulated notion of improvement that functions primarily to make compositionists 'feel' as though they are working with their students' best interests at heart. Such 'improvement' operates only under a guise of making students' writing better, serving, instead, as purveyor of institutional politics" (Dobrin 2011, 12).[6] Perhaps it is because of the field's intense focus on pedagogy and student learning that composition theorists tend to dismiss the activities of their own field, but it is rare to hear participants in other university disciplines express such a negative perception of their own endeavors, and what is so strange about this situation is that composition is a field that tries to examine and improve its pedagogical methods on a regular basis. Should we call this *disciplinary self-hatred* or are the frustrations being expressed about composition teaching and research a displaced reflection on the problems facing higher education in general? In a version of capitalist realism, since people do not believe there is any alternative to the current system, all they can do is critique it and repeat it in a process of cynical conformity.[7]

CYNICAL CONFORMITY IN WRITING STUDIES

Cynical conformity is defined by the fact that people conform to a system in which they no longer believe, and we can see how many of the self-critical attitudes concerning composition may stem from this type of social subjectivity, which many see as a dominant form of being in neoliberal late capitalism.

According to the logic of austerity, we will never have enough money to support workers and public institutions in the same way we did in the past, so all we can do is fight over a shrinking amount of resources.[8] Moreover, as society becomes more unequal and the competition for a decreasing number of good jobs increases, people double down on competing within the dominant system. However, at the same time everyone tries to get ahead, they also know the system is rigged and mobility is difficult to attain; the result is that people must find a way to work hard in the current system while they judge it in a critical way from a position of distance and noninvolvement. Thus, to keep the self pure and innocent, all evil must be located externally, and here people become split between their hatred of the system and their conformity to it.[9] In short, when people do not organize to change the system, they can only critique and repeat it through cynical conformity.

In Dobrin's case, his contradictory position in relation to composition is that he wants theory to be privileged above all else, but he also realizes that the very institutions privileging theory debase teaching, writing, learning, and students. Since he cannot have it both ways, he ends up turning his anger away from the system and redirecting it toward the oppressed victims of the system:

> On the surface, the field works toward improvement, but such "improvement" might be better interpreted as "civilizing" or even "humanizing" or, more accurately, "colonizing." As Crowley so rightly points out, this "improvement" is also a veil for creating a universal student subjectivity and for institutionalizing the parameters of what that subjectivity is to be—or to be more precise, for actually producing that subjectivity (as product) based on institutionally set parameters. To this end, composition studies' work toward improvement is, of course, sanctioned by the institution because it operates as an institutional control mechanism. No matter the standard that composition studies flies proclaiming critical consciousness, liberatory learning, literacy, or other "emancipatory" practices, these "methods" are confirmed by the institution as valid methods of initiating students into institutional discourses. (Dobrin 2011, 12)

In many ways, this passage highlights a backlash discourse in which the efforts to teach students certain progressive models of education are seen as being oppressive attempts to impose a colonizing discourse on the poor helpless students. In contrast to this view, I argue that composition classes are some of the only places where the dominant paradigm of the research university is challenged and students are given a space to think outside and beyond the standard academic structure of lecturing, note taking, and testing; however, the problem is that the potentially liberating effects of composition courses are undermined by the dominant educational structures that surround these isolated classes.

Like the right-wing critics who argue that liberal professors are trying to control their students by indoctrinating them into a left-wing ideology, Dobrin sees efforts to engage students in composition classes as a secret way to control them:[10] "What is wrong, however, a la Gilles Deleuze and Felix Guattari, is that such 'improvement' serves not to emancipate students but to 'reterritorialize' them into positions more easily controlled" (Dobrin 2011, 13). The problem with this theory is that it does not leave any space for a critical mode of teaching writing, as it ends up replicating the destructive backlash attacks on political correctness.

While we should value theory and the way it can be used to expand and challenge our views of the world, Dobrin's employment of theory appears to be grounded in an effort to use it as an ideal object, which makes everything else seem impure and tainted. For example, after extolling the virtues of pure theory, he makes the following cynical claim about the field of composition:

> What is even more bothersome—if not ethically abhorrent—is composition studies' masking of its institutional missions as agendas of improvement and doing so with little, if any, critical examination of the work toward improvement. Casting such work as positive, as helping students become "better," allows compositionists to divest themselves of the responsibility of having to take into consideration in any critical way their own

roles in colonizing students, since such approaches are, compositionists tell themselves, methods for resisting the very system in which they operate. This is, of course, an easy way to rationalize the field's role in such institutionally colonizing acts. (Dobrin 2011, 13)

This claim that the field of composition never looks at itself in a critical fashion because it is so invested in its fake discourse of student improvement is often disproven by the overly self-critical tendencies of the field I have highlighted.

In fact, Dobrin's own criticism of composition practices seems to be highly generalized and overly negative. For instance, the following passage provides a deeply cynical interpretation of the entire discipline:

As Kenneth Burke so plainly puts it: "The shepherd, qua shepherd, acts for the good of the sheep, to protect them from discomfiture and harm. But he may be 'identified' with a project that is raising the sheep for market" (27) After all, institutional support for composition studies will always be there—departments will continue to hire compositionists and students will be required to take composition courses—as long as composition studies research remains devoted to its pedagogical methods, methods that simply cheer on the institutional mission, no matter what compositionists tell themselves. Theory attached to classroom practice is necessarily, always already co-opted and cannot, by definition, be emancipatory since classroom practice is sanctioned by the institution. Thus, any hope of real emancipatory work in theory, in composition studies, must be disassociated from the classroom. To this end, too, investing in research methods that derive from classroom practice, composition studies is able to avoid doing the difficult work of theory in favor of doing the easier work of the institution, work that is funded and sanctioned and that provides objects of study—students—at the ready. All of these factors contribute to composition studies' resistance to theoretical work. Because composition/writing theory does not always (immediately) work toward improving students' writing in any easy, identifiable manner, many compositionists do not see theoretical work as having any bearing on the mission of the field's research. Composition theory is resisted because it does not work to the end of "improvement" in any tangible way. (Dobrin 2011, 13)

Dobrin posits here that composition scholars avoid doing theory because it is much easier to teach students and research how
students learn than to develop a discourse void of institutional
concerns. He also feels writing faculty are somehow preparing
their students for slaughter, but those faculty deny this because
they have bought into their own claims about improving students. Once again, at the very moment Dobrin appears to be
making a radical call for change, he is actually reinforcing the
dominant research-university paradigm.

Although I have argued that writing studies does tend to
support a discourse of social conformity, there is little sign that
this stress on helping students succeed in and out of school
is nothing more than the result of not organizing to change
the oppressive structures of our education system. Within the
classroom, many compositionists do try to challenge the dominant paradigm, but they are so focused on local issues they
do not take on the larger structural forces. However, my criticism of the field is coupled with a valorization of what many
composition teachers are trying to do in the classroom. Thus,
the attention to students, learning, writing, practice, and form
should be supported, but these aspects of education will be
debased by a system that privileges theory, research, graduate
education, and administration.

Dobrin seems to favor a university without students, so he
continues to berate composition scholars who focus on student
subjectivity and agency: "The focus, then, of composition studies has been one directed not at writing but at subjects and the
administration of those subjects. Composition studies is more
interested in issues of subjectivity and agency than in writing"
(Dobrin 2011, 13). On one level, Dobrin wants to affirm a mode
of discourse that is networked and posthuman, and on another
level, the elimination of concerns for student writing and subjectivity does clear a space for the pure theorist who need not
waste time teaching or grading students papers or meeting with
students to conference over their work.[11]

Dobrin's efforts to expand the ways we think about writing
pushes him to conclude that for the field of composition, the

only types of writers under consideration are novice subjects, and this focus is chosen because people in composition like to colonize and control young people from a position of expertise: "In a discipline that focuses primarily on classrooms, writing-subjects are (re) formulated as student-subjects, the implication being that these are novice subjects, not-yet-fully-formed subjects, inexperienced subjects, subjects in need of training, in need of making" (Dobrin 2011, 14). Once again, what Dobrin is describing is more appropriate to an analysis of many other fields and disciplines since composition has been one of the only fields to question the academic hierarchy that privileges expert faculty over novice student. Instead of taking on this larger structural target, Dobrin obsessively turns his criticism to his own field and repeats the neoconservative claim that universities are simply factories for liberal indoctrination.

Part of this backlash discourse is a conservative reaction to the postmodern educational stress on the ways people are shaped by larger social and cultural forces:

> Concepts such as culture, ideology, discourse, and language all become central to the composition studies conversation as the vehicles through which subjectivity is formed/produced. The work of the field becomes both an examination of and a pedagogy of reading how those forces play upon student subjectivity. Often in the name of rhetorical analysis, this is the work of interpretation of texts/artifacts in order to better see how those texts affect individual subjectivities so that those subjects might be better empowered to react to those forces. Sanchez's work and Susan Miller's "Technologies of Self?-Formation" make clear that such an approach to understanding subject-formation is essentially the work of interpretation and that such approaches deny students—or at least deny that students have—the power to write the very artifacts of their own subjectivities. (Dobrin 2011, 14)

In another turn of the screw, Dobrin now appears to be arguing that the focus on social and ideological determination in composition classes serves to deny students their own subjectivity and agency, yet many of his own previous statements call for not thinking about agency or subjectivity. One reason for this contradiction is that Dobrin is repeating the classic neoliberal

argument that people are not determined by larger social, political, and economic forces; instead, individuals are able turn to
new media and create their own culture through acts of appro-
priation and remixing.

THE LIBERTARIAN CYBERCULTURE

It is likely Dobrin considers himself a left-wing radical, but his
arguments show a conformity with right-wing discourse. This
combination of opposing ideologies is often found in contemporary culture, in part due to our desire to simply imagine away
the hierarchies and oppositions structuring our daily existence.
Furthermore, this combination of the radical Left and dominant Right also points to the underlying bipartisan acceptance
of the neoliberal discourse, and one of the main tenants of this
ideology is a focus on bottom-up, decentralized networks. Just
as the Left recently had its populist movement in the form of
the decentralized Occupy Wall Street, the Right also had its sup-
posedly bottom-up, decentralized Tea Party. One common trait
of these opposing wings is that there is a strong neoanarchist
and libertarian vibe, and this ideology also feeds into the way
theorists like Dobrin see the World Wide Web as a bottom-up,
decentralized network without traditional power structures or
control centers.[12]

Dobrin's critique of the subject in composition can be best
understand by thinking about the libertarian privileging of
markets and networks over government intervention. Fredrick
Hayek (1945), one of the founding fathers of libertarian, neoliberal economics was fond of saying that since no single person
has enough knowledge of the economy, the market must figure
things out by matching supply and demand.[13] Hayek saw free
markets as bottom-up, decentralized networks where no one
individual has enough knowledge, and this lack of knowledge
means experts and government officials must be questioned.
Hayek's work thus anticipated the current interest in the wis-
dom of the crowds and distributed knowledge, and it is this
combination of markets and networks that gives insight into

Dobrin's formulations of posthuman subjectivity: "The conceptions of subjectivity upon which composition studies has relied no longer accurately explain the location or function of subjectivity or agency within the networked, hyper-circulatory, complex situation of writing in which we now find ourselves" (Dobrin 2011, 77). Since people now often write on networks and through networks, the older model of media and subjectivity no longer holds for Dobrin, and like Hayek, this rethinking of the subject repositions our relationship to knowledge and authority: "While most thinking in posthumanism does not reject the rationalism tied to humanism, posthumanism does critique the role of the autonomous thinker and casts human thought as imperfect and not the avenue through which the world is known or defined" (61). It is then this conception of the subject's limited knowledge and control in networked culture that brings together the free-market, antigovernment rhetoric of the Right's and the Left's desire for a nonhierarchical, decentralized social structure.

Like the Silicon Valley promoters of flat organizations and open platforms, neoliberal libertarians on the right and the left turn to an idealized view of social networks to critique any form of traditional hierarchy and bureaucracy. What many libertarians on the left do not fully appreciate though is that this rejection of modern and premodern notions of subjectivity and knowledge results in a call to reject all governmental interventions in the economy.[14] Since only the networked market can sort through and match all of our individual choices, government planners can only impose their will from a position of ignorance. From Dobrin's perspective, networked culture also downgrades the dominant role of humans: "Many posthumanisms work to realign humans not as superior to other species but as operating as any other species; in doing so, posthumanism denies humanity an ethical superiority above nature and, more important, sees humanity as not operating somehow above or outside encompassing systems: biological, ecological, technological, or other" (Dobrin 2011, 61). This displacement of the human subject from the center of its own creations can have both positive and negative effects. On the one hand, it could force us to see we are not in control of nature and must learn to live within natural constraints; on the other hand, this decentering of the subject can undermine our ability to work collectively to fix any problems.

This neoliberal libertarian discourse also calls into question any expert and promotes a cult of the amateur as we see in many new media networks. An unintended result of this downgrading of expertise is that experts, like professors, are downsized and casualized. Of course, these material considerations rarely show up in the rhetoric of the posthumanist cyberoptimists; instead, their discourse is often one of radical conformity, which can be seen in the following passage by Dobrin:

> Posthumanism is influenced by—if not triggered by—the changes imposed on the human by things like genetic manipulation, cybernetics, artificial intelligence, psychotropic pharmaceuticals, and other biotechnical research. Ultimately, posthumanism is defined by a kind of amorphous understanding of core human alteration brought about by some interaction with technology: biological, electric/digital, or chemical (pharmaceutical, for instance). (Dobrin 2011, 62)

Although some people might want to critique the effects drugs and computer technologies are having on people, Dobrin's perspective appears to be value free on this subject. In fact, while Dobrin repeats the conservative caricature of liberal professors oppressing their students by indoctrinating them with left-wing ideology, he appears to give a free pass to the pharmaceutical and computer corporations: "This popular posthumanist (sometimes transhumanist) discourse structures the research agendas of much of corporate biotechnology and informatics as well as serving as a legitimating narrative for new social entities (cyborgs, artificial intelligence, and virtual societies) composed of fundamentally fluid, flexible, and changeable identities. For popular posthumanism, the future is a space for the realization of individuality, the transcendence of biological limits, and the creation of a new social order" (63). In this speculative order of high theory, the desire to transcend material limitations leads to an acceptance of the biotechno-logical manipulation of human beings.

The promoters of new technologies often fall into this trap of arguing that we are entering a new age in which all the past categories and relationships will no longer matter. Therefore, if we can download our consciousness into the network and take a drug to stay awake all hours of the day and night, we no longer experience any physical or mental limitations. Thus, cyberuto-pianism also feeds a promotion of the unregulated free market because the network and the market follow the same basic logic; here, the freedom from the limitations of the self and the body replicate the ideology of the individual freed from governmen-tal intervention or social compromise: "Likewise, information technology interventions such as networked space or wearable/portable devices that link users to information exchange sys-tems render the human more akin to Donna J. Haraway's con-cept of cyborg, Bruno Latour's concept of the hybrid, or even, perhaps, Teilhard de Chardin's concept of noosphere. Central to comprehending posthuman subjectivity, critical posthuman-ism understands the posthuman to be able to perpetually shift identities" (65). Just as capitalism now enters and restructures all our fundamental social relations and institutions, including higher education, the networked subject shows no resistance to manipulation by the market/network: capital flow and finan-cialization become confused with subjective fluidity.

In terms of composition, Dobrin uses this notion of the decentered, fluid subject as a way of countering the more tradi-tional notion of subjectivity still found in writing studies: "The posthuman, to borrow from Gilles Deleuze and Felix Guattari, is in a perpetual state of becoming. Composition studies has traditionally relied upon knowing the subject as fixed, a sub-ject more commonly associated with Enlightenment thinking" (Dobrin 2011, 65). When the subject is unfixed, there no lon-ger can be a stable teacher or student in the teacher-student relationship; instead, a flux of writing circulates among differ-ent networks and environments. It is interesting how this con-ception of subjectivity fits in so well with the flexible worker of post-Fordist ideology.[15] In other terms, the theoretical celebration of the destabilized subject matches the way workers are being transformed into contingent free agents moving from one disloyal employer to the next or plugging into a network of part-time, just-in-time gigs. This radical discourse can therefore be considered to be just a theoretical idealization of our downsized status quo.

In a culture in which private equity firms melt away large companies in the blink of an eye, and most faculty do not know whether they will ever be hired back, we are told to embrace the fluid nature of networked capitalism. Meanwhile, we are also admonished for still believing in the value of individual students and individual faculty members and the quest to give both of them some level of stability in their lives:

> A postmodern concept of a fluctuating subject has been difficult for composition studies simply because no matter the openness to postmodern thinking about subjectivity, composition studies manages to reduce the postmodern shift of subject to a codifiable, recognizable subject that can be identified as somehow operating outside of writing—still a subject. The posthuman, on the other hand, should be seen not as outside of writing but as an integrated part of writing, of the whole, shifting like the postmodern subject, certainly, but able to flow and redefine as the surrounding environment demands it or imposes it. How the posthuman finds itself in such a condition is central to the work of posthumanism. (Dobrin 2011, 65)

Part of the problem with this passage, and many other discussions of posthumanism and postmodernism, is that these two concepts are conflated. Postmodernism is best understood as the period following modernity, and not only did this cultural moment critique the limitations and exclusions of modern universality, but we must think of this critique in relation to the rise of minority social movements and the invention of the welfare state. This postmodernism of the Left is often confused with the purely aesthetic and theoretical postmodernism of the academic neoliberal consensus. Posthumanism then falls into the latter category and is most often a backlash against postmodern social movements for justice and democratic emancipation. In this sense, Dobrin's criticisms of the attempt of composition teachers to see their work as political and ideological falls into the posthuman rejection of postmodernity.

It is important to separate the postmodern social movements of the 1960s from the current celebration of networks, fluid subjectivity, and posthumanism. For instance, MOOCs have been sold to the public as offering students total control, as the students are all plugged into the same predetermined network distributing the same information. Thus, consumers are told they are now free to buy whatever they want whenever they want it, but they must buy the same things from the same global source. In this cultural context, freedom is the ultimate value, and not only do we want our speech to be free from censorship and control, but we want all information and entertainment to be free of charge. According to Dobrin, we also want to free ourselves from our bodies, degeneration, and self-control:

> While many popular posthumanists argue for brain augmentations, pharmaceutical interventions to mask or eliminate mental constraints such as depression, or amplification through technological body enhancements like prosthetic devices incorporated into the human to create the cyborg, others see these same interventions as potentially extending not just the human experience but human life spans. Some extend such visions to the extent of immortality through pharmaceutical and biotechnological replacement or even the possibility of consciousness uploading, an idea that suggests human thought and consciousness can be measured and transferred to other housing bodies, like computer memories, allowing the individual the possibility of perpetual eternal upload. (Dobrin 2011, 66)

What is so strange is that this utopian attempt to free ourselves from our own bodies and minds is based on a fundamentally pessimistic view of human knowledge. After all, it is because we do not know enough on our own that we must plug into the hive to crowd source our knowledge in the market of ideas.

Like so much of American culture, posthumanism is bent on escaping death and aging, and this escape requires moving beyond our modern notion of the body:[16] "As Hayles explains: 'When information loses its body, equating humans and computers is especially easy, for the materiality in which the thinking mind is instantiated appears incidental to its essential nature'" (Dobrin 2011, 67). This desire to equate the mind with a computer by dislodging the body reflects the current reductive notion of the self as a technological system open to mechanical manipulation and improvement. If the brain is a computer, the computer is the brain, and there is no need for human consciousness, freedom, intentionality, and ambivalence. Furthermore, if the brain is a computer, I can be programmed and reprogrammed, and my relation to my computer can be as important as my relation to other people.

Marx's theory that in capitalism, people will treat other people like things and things like people is alive and well, and when all entities are subjected to the cash nexus, they no longer have any stable identity or limits: everything solid really does melt in the air when technology and theory mediate the subject by networks and markets. In the posthuman discourse of cybercapitalism, all entities are locked into a constant feedback loop of mediation and information: "Likewise, the concept of the feedback loop, a concept we shall see as central to systems theories and complexity theories, 'implies that the boundaries of the autonomous subject are up for grabs, since feedback loops can flow not only within the subject but also between the subject and the environment'"(67). This turn to posthumanism in writing studies represents the ultimate attempt to circumvent material, political, economic, and institutional concerns by creating a fluid space for networked subjectivity and writing:

> The posthuman is characterized by four key assumptions: First, the posthuman view privileges informational pattern over material instantiation, so that embodiment in a biological substrate is seen as an accident over history rather than an inevitability of life. Second, the posthuman view considers consciousness, regarded as the seat of human identity in the Western tradition long before Descartes thought he was a mind thinking, as an epiphenomenon, as an evolutionary upstart trying to claim that it is the whole show when in actuality it is only a minor sideshow. Third, the posthuman view thinks of the body as the original prosthesis we all learn to manipulate, so that extending

or replacing the body with other prostheses becomes a continuation of a process that began before we were born. Fourth, and most important, by these and other means, the posthuman view configures human being so that it can be seamlessly articulated with intelligent machines. In the posthuman, there are no essential differences or absolute demarcations between bodily existence and computer simulation, cybernetic mechanism and biological organism, robot teleology and human goals. (Dobrin 2011, 68)

Just as the neoliberal ideology cleared a space for the dominance of free markets by undermining the role of governmental planning and intervention, the posthumanists envision a world devoid of material constraints. Here the Hegelian intellectual dialectic has taken charge: material relations are repressed and replaced by a spiritual synthesis of opposites.

Of course, one of the fundamental oppositions wished away by the posthuman is the conflict between the self and the other, which mimics the tension between the individual and society: "The idea that the subject maintains 'agency, desire, or will' that can be distinguished from the 'will of others' is 'undercut in the posthuman, for the posthuman's collective heterogeneous quality implies a distributed cognition located in disparate parts that may be in only tenuous communication with one another'" (Dobrin 2011, 69) Just as advertisers sell people the idea of free choice, posthumanism tries to eliminate the individual and the social by creating a space for the mass individual in the form of networked subjectivity.

The turn toward high theory therefore allows for a superficial overcoming of the social hierarchies that shape our world. For example, in the following discussion of Marc Hansen's work, Dobrin celebrates the way all the classic oppositions structuring the modern world are now being transcended through posthumanism:

> What Hansen also does is provide the posthumanist thinker with a more integrated vision of the technological/human amalgam beyond mere augmentation, a concept that emphasizes a central object/ body that is transformed by the addition or alteration of parts rather than a concept that sees the central objects/body as

being integrated to the extent that the parts render a new whole. When Picard is assimilated by the Borg, we still see Picard—his identifiableness continues. But integration suggests a way of identifying the whole rather than its constitutive parts. The bond between the human and material technology is recast as inseparable and the posthuman as both inevitable and achieved. Yes, resistance is futile; you will be/have been assimilated. (Dobrin 2011, 72)

In this discourse of total assimilation, any resistance is seen as being futile; in other words, there is no alternative to the current system, and all we can do is go along for the ride. Of course this lack of alternative is one of the driving forces behind neoliberal ideology. In the age of austerity, everyone must accept that there is no alternative to our current capitalist system.

In many ways, Dobrin's work reveals the ways new media technologies are helping naturalize free-market ideology by making all resistance appear to be foolish and futile: "Given composition studies' focus on student writing-subjects and that those subjects are inseparable from technology—for composition students embroiled in the culture of corporate America, this is easily identifiable in the pervasiveness of wearable and integrated information technology devices—we can no longer address writing-subjects, student or other, as subjects but instead must begin to consider the posthuman position (or at minimum transhuman)" (Dobrin 2011, 72). The rhetoric of posthumanism then pushes us to submit to the corporate culture's promotion of ubiquitous technologies, and since composition considers writing as reliant on technology, writing studies must embrace this neoliberal order.

In a culture in which technology and free-market capitalism remediate all our fundamental relationships, Dobrin urges composition faculty to stop thinking about individuals, students, consciousness, and agency:

As composition theorists, if we work in the realm of agents, subjects or consciousness, then our descriptions of writing will only ever present it as an instrument, as a means by which something else is arrived at. But if we give up the deep-seated and ultimate unfounded assumption that writing is a function and product of individuals interacting with the world, with culture, with tradition, or even with themselves, then we might begin to address the many implications of the proposition that writing is a phenomenon of constant (re)circulation, one that promises the representation of something else but never actually delivers. (Dobrin 2011, 73)

By seeing writing as an activity of constant recirculation and deferral, the roles of student and teacher are melted away, as a system of total exchange is implemented: "Current thinking about subjectivity clearly unfolds ideas that subjectivity in the new media era is produced as a collective, media-driven subjectivity, and posthumanist thinking acutely critiques any concept of the individual subject in light of numerous technologies, including informational and biological. . . . Likewise, systems theories and complexity theories question the very possibility of an autonomous subject" (Dobrin 2011, 74). Although one could interpret this turn to posthumanism in writing studies as a renewed focus on composition as a social process, Dobrin seeks to extinguish the social and the individual at the same time: "Composition studies' attention to student subjects and its eagerness for normalized intellectual activity, FYC curriculum, and managerial oversight indicts composition studies as partner in larger political and institutional actions that actually deny subjectivity in favor of a normalized collective" (Dobrin 2011, 74). From the perspective of neoliberal cyberlibertarianism, any attempt at collective action is a form of bureaucratic imposition. In this context, teachers of composition are simply a tool for the administrative colonization of student subjects: "No matter how you slice it, administrative, institutional, curricular, and political normalizing can only be code for homogenization. One of the primary tasks of postcomposition is to work away from such normalizing efforts in order to dodge composition studies' enchantment with subjectivity, primarily as resistant members of the discipline" (Dobrin 2011, 74). Since resistance is futile in the posthuman network, any indication of subjective agency must be read as a false representation hiding a deeper, administrative control.

The cynicism of Dobrin's perspective is derived in part from the loss of social trust in a system sustained by naturalized inequality. Since we know our social structures are unfair and unjust, and we do not think we can do anything to change them, all we can do is conform from a cynical distance. For Dobrin, the idealization of the posthuman network creates a space for critiquing the system from a position of uninvolved innocence. In other terms, his presentation of an alternative view of subjectivity and society removes him from direct involvement in the system he is criticizing. Of course, this idealized position is impossible and can only be achieved through a mental leap into pure theory.

Once Dobrin establishes the new purified posthuman order, he returns to composition to argue that the field is corrupted by the need to cash in on students:

> We must first acknowledge that the primacy of the student subject in composition studies results not from a genuine disciplinary interest in students as subjects, in students as writers, or even in subjects in general but grows from the simple fact that subjects are the primary capital of composition studies. And, in saying so, we can easily see how composition studies' conservatism grows from a desire to control that capital. It is, we must admit, much easier to identify and control this capital, particularly when the field retains the right of subjectification of the student under the guise of writing instruction, than it is to control something as amorphous and problematic as writing. Subjects are the economy of composition studies, and part of the field's encumbrance in this economy is its historic/bureaucratic adherence to economy rather than to (or at least not in conjunction with) ecology. (Dobrin 2011, 74).

The argument here is that the entire field of composition is driven by the need to control students because they represent capital for writing programs, and therefore if writing studies adopted a networked, posthuman theory of writing, it would not need to control anything because everything would be part of the same ecological system of recirculation.

The paradox of Dobrin's position is that at the very moment he ascribes to the new capitalist order of free-market networks, he attacks composition for only caring about students as a source of capital: "Composition studies' adherence to economic models has forced the field to value academic pursuits—those that deal in the capital of the institution, the students—over intellectual pursuits that often ignore the confine of capital in favor of the movement of speculation and possibility" (Dobrin 2011, 75). At first reading, one may think Dobrin is offering a radical critique of the replacement of learning with the cash nexus, but his investment in markets, networks, and new media technologies shows he is simply favoring the new model of financialized, post-Fordist capitalism over the older model of industrial capitalism.[17] The use of the term *speculation* is important here because it stands not only for pure theory but also for the speculative nature of our financialized economy.

As he speculates about the capitulation of composition to administrative capitalism, he also affirms that the field has no choice because there is no possible alternative: "Though I criticize composition studies for entrenching itself in economic approaches over ecological approaches, it is probably unreasonable to suggest that the discipline has the power to actually make such decisions in the application of its work (teaching), even if it can in the abstraction of its work (theory), without the literal permission of the college, the university, and the state legislature" (Dobrin 2011, 75). Although Dobrin offers this analysis as proof there is no alternative and resistance is futile, my argument is that he is right: we do need to realize nothing will change unless we organize to take on the college, the university, and the state legislature.

Like so many other theorists of writing studies, instead of making a call for collective action and political intervention, Dobrin retreats to the safe confines of theoretical speculation: "This is an actual rescuing of the subject by not allowing the perpetual manipulation and normalization of student subjects by the academy and instead freeing the subject into a constant process of becoming" (Dobrin 2011, 75). In gesturing to a questionable reading of Nietzsche and Deleuze, Dobrin sees change as only occurring through an intellectual reimagining of the present. Part of this new present is a world without subjects, identity, resistance, and individuality: "Without subjectivity, many may argue, we lose individuality, the opportunity for resistance, identity, and other opportunities for each of us—or more accurately, each of our students—to find position in the world exclusive to each. But such ideas are holdovers from romantic notions of Enlightenment thinking that the individual subject is unique, identifiable (even if only self-identifiable), and somehow of value" (Dobrin 2011, 75). While it is important to question the focus on individual rewards in our education system, it is hard to imagine how we can simply wish away individuality, but for Dobrin, this loss of the subject is required to reimagine writing itself: "The removal of subject from the scene of writing confirms that it is not who writes that is important but that writing is there" (Dobrin 2011, 76). By detaching writing from identity and individuality, he is able to argue that resistance only occurs in writing itself and not through the intentions of subjects: "Disruption is inherent in the mechanism of writing (see Zizek; Badiou; Derrida); it is not the intent of the subject. Writing resists" (76). Paul de Man has affirmed that the resistance to theory is inherent to theory, but Dobrin wants to argue that resistance only resides in the posthuman network of recirculation: "By seeing writing not as the product (or process) of a producing subject but as a never-ending (re) circulation in which larger producing/desiring machines generate and perpetuate writing throughout network, system, and environment, we are better able to attend to the issue of writing and circulation as primary to the theoretical work of postcomposition" (77). In the integrated network linking machine and human and subject and other, writing is defined by its ability to circulate within the system. Once again, this vision is not critical or disruptive because it is based on the notion that there is nothing outside the capitalist system: "Or, to be more direct, we can say that it does not matter whether one considers oneself to be posthuman or not because we live in a posthuman world. In all instances, degrees of posthuman augmentation are controlled by capital" (87). The final gesture in this analysis is thus to reaffirm that there is no way to block this restructuring of our lives by capital and technology. Like students constantly texting each other during class, we are encouraged to give up all resistance and engage in the endless recirculation of writing.

What is so strange is that this promotion of new media-networked posthumanism is coupled with an insightful critique of this new cultural order. For example, Dobrin reveals the problem of naturalizing new technologies: "The energy reaction results not from the ubiquity of a technology but from its invisibility, its ability to naturalize itself as not-technology. The predominant characteristic of technology's ability to form the cyborg, the hybrid, the posthuman is its invisibility, not its ubiquity" (89). Dobrin is correct here in stressing that the power of many new technologies rests in their invisibility, which allows them to be folded seamlessly into our lives. This invisibility, in turn, serves to naturalize social construction and artificial machines, but this critical insight is transcended by the idea that there can be no subject positioned outside this system to make this criticism. Thus, once again, resistance and criticism are futile because there is nothing external to the constant recirculation of the network.

In referring to the work of Katherine Hayles, Dobrin posits that with the posthuman, we no longer can think in terms of wealth, power, and individuals:

> The posthuman does not really mean the end of humanity. It signals instead the end of a certain conception that may have applied, at best, to that fraction of humanity who still had wealth, power, and leisure to conceptualize themselves as autonomous beings exercising their will through individual agency and choice. What is lethal is not the posthuman as such but the grafting of the posthuman onto a liberal humanist view of the self. (Dobrin 2011, 90)

It is hard to imagine anyone but a secure academic thinker being able to wish away the critical categories of wealth, power, and individuality: in fact, it is this detachment from reality that is coupled with a desire to escape the mundane duties of teaching students, grading their writing, and administering an academic program. Without a subject and a notion of individuality, there can be no way to hold anyone accountable to their teaching duties, and this voiding of academic obligations may be one of the goals of affirming the posthuman present.

Not only does Dobrin push for composition without administration, students, and identity, but he also calls for the field to simply ignore its evident labor problem:

> While composition studies may be ethically bound to continue seeking solutions for the uncomfortable situation of contingent labor in writing instruction by improving the conditions of those contingent laborers, postcomposition disavows these conversations because they are not beneficial to furthering any understanding of the phenomena of writing or the position of writing studies in the academy. Postcomposition adopts a position that arguments about contingent labor have been influenced by a focus on subjects rather than upon the systems and ecologies of those systems in which subjects believe they require agency. (Dobrin 2011, 117)

From Dobrin's perspective, the exploitation of contingent labor in composition programs should be simply disavowed because, after all, these workers are only subjects seeking some kind of agency. This argument should make it clear that this turn to theory is founded on a desire to simply repress the material relations shaping the field.

NOTES

1. On one level, we can see Dobrin as rejecting the types of social conformity I have located in the work of other writing studies specialists. However, on another level, he calls for us to conform to the dominant research-university paradigm that places theory over practice.

2. Like many of the other theorists discuss in this book, Dobrin tends to veil conformity to neoliberal ideology under the cloak of critique and self-awareness. For example, his turn to a networked theory of subjectivity replicates the ways we are all subjected to markets and communication structures in contemporary culture. For a radical critique of this culture, see Douglas Kellner (2002).

3. For a more radical critique of administration in composition, see Bousquet (2008).

4. My critique of writing studies theory and speculative solutions follows Marx's critique of Hegel. As Marx (1975) shows, within the structure of

the dialectic, material conflicts are overcome by mental combinations. Moreover, as Louis Althusser (2006) has argued, ideology represents the imaginary mediation of real relations.

5. In reading Dobrin's criticism of Smit (2004), it becomes clear to me that my own criticism of genre theory could be misinterpreted as an attack on the field itself and the need to teach students how to write in particular situations. Unlike Dobrin, my critique is centered on revaluing the importance of teaching students the practice of writing. Moreover, I do not see my own discourse as antitheory; instead, I am focused on using theory to critique certain tendencies in writing studies.

6. Once again, Dobrin's self-consuming critique of composition could be seen as similar to my own criticism of writing studies. However, my focus is on the need for institutional change to match the best practices of current composition courses.

7. This reference to capitalist realism is restating Fisher's (2009) argument that since we see no alternative to capitalism, all we can do is conform to the current system in a cynical way.

8. For the history of this rhetoric of austerity in higher education, see Newfield 2008.

9. Magill (2009) offers an insightful reading of the ways cynicism and irony allow people to critique a system while remaining pure and innocent.

10. For a classic right-wing attack on left-wing professors, see David Horowitz (2012).

11. For an analysis of the vexed relationship among teaching, writing, and theory, see Samuels (2013, 43–57).

12. Fred Turner (2010) discusses the ways the 1960s counterculture has blended in with the new computer culture through a shared libertarian ideology.

13. In "The Use of Knowledge in Society," Hayek (1945) anticipated new media networks and neoliberal economics.

14. William Easterly's (2014) *The Tyranny of Experts* displays a growing libertarian consensus that calls into question expert knowledge and the welfare state.

15. For an analysis of the post-Fordist worker, see Bob Jessop (1993).

16. Christopher Lasch's (1998) *The Culture of Narcissism* argues that American culture is driven by the desire to escape death.

17. For the neoliberal financialization of higher education, see Kirp (2009) and Readings (1996).

CONCLUSION
Collective Action to Reinvent the University

Throughout this book, I have been highlighting how many scholars in writing studies have done a good job of analyzing the economic and political issues facing higher education in general and composition in particular, but this analysis has not been connected to any real plan for structural transformation. Even though some people have argued for effective ways to promote local change, the general consensus appears to be that there is no real alternative to our current system of education. In order to provide some hope and knowledge about how change is possible, I want to examine several actions that can be undertaken to reinvent the university from the bottom.

CONFRONTING HIERARCHIES

As I have argued, contemporary institutions of higher education tend to be structured by a series of social hierarchies placing research over teaching, theory over practice, content over form, reading over writing, the sciences over the humanities, and graduate education over undergraduates. Since composition is often equated with teaching undergraduates a basic formal skill, it is placed in a debased position within this system. In order to counter this problem, many proponents of writing studies have argued that if the discipline can produce its own respected research, more resources and tenure-track lines will be provided for composition. I have argued that this strategy represents a cynical conformity with the present system because instead of changing things, it tries to succeed in a discredited system.

In order to stop trying to conform to the dominant research-university paradigm that affects many different types of institutions, I argue that we must use collective action to fight for a

DOI: 10.7330/9781607325840.c006

different institutional structure, and one glimmer of hope for this type of transformation can be found in the recent increase in efforts to unionize contingent faculty throughout the country.[1] Since the vast majority of people teaching writing in higher education today are non-tenure-track faculty, the process of organizing contingent faculty has the potential to transform composition and universities from below.[2] However, in order for real structural change to take place, it will be necessary to tie the process of unionizing contingent faculty to larger curricular and institutional transformations. In short, unions must promote a new model of higher education by reclaiming the importance of undergraduate education at research universities, and one reason unions are so essential to this process is that it is necessary to find a collective force that can counter the administrative drive to reinforce structural hierarchies.

As president of the contingent faculty union at the University of California, I have seen how an organized group of mostly undergraduate faculty can use their collective resources and power to promote teaching, undergraduate education, and non-tenure-track faculty. Part of this process has been to use our negotiating rights to bargain over educational issues like student evaluations, professional development, shared governance, class size, merit reviews, and promotion criteria.[3] I have also taught in two writing programs staffed primarily by unionized full-time, non-tenure-track faculty, and these programs have increased the level of workplace democracy by fighting against many forms of educational hierarchy.

If the growing trend of organizing non-tenure-track faculty continues, and if there is an effort to tie organizing to educational issues, it is possible to imagine a reinvention of the university from below. There are many *ifs* in this statement, but my own experience has shown that organized faculty can push institutions to pay more attention to how they fund and support undergraduate education. In the case of my union, UC-AFT, we represent over five thousand non-tenure-track faculty in the University of California system, and we are known for having one of the best contracts in the country for contingent faculty. While there is still plenty of room for improvement, at one of the largest public university systems in the country, activism and organization have led to a model that could be replicated throughout the United States.[4] Even in states that bar collective bargaining, contingent faculty can still form unions and other collective organizations. Moreover, when unions increase the standards at their own institutions, such strides can affect nonunionized institutions by redefining the labor and educational norms.

BEYOND CONTINGENCY

One of the first things that should happen is that universities and colleges must be forced to give up their dependence on insecure, part-time labor. This goal can be partially achieved by moving to a system of long-term contracts for contingent faculty. Another aspect of this transformation would be to require a limit on the number of student credit hours taught by part-time instructors and graduate students. Contracts that prioritize full-time work can be used to make teaching more stable and professional since many part-time faculty hired at the last minute do not have sufficient time to prepare for their courses. Also, a move to more secure positions would put pressure on institutions to hire people in a more thoughtful manner, which could also push departments to only employ people with the requisite expertise and experience. The idea here is that we must move away from the notion that anyone can teach undergraduate courses like first-year composition, and one way to do make that move is to create more stable and full-time positions.

Another key to changing the working conditions of non-tenure-track faculty in composition and beyond is the creation of a comprehensive model for reviewing faculty for promotion, merit, and reappointment. Too many universities and colleges rely solely on student evaluations to evaluate non-tenure-track faculty, so it is necessary to motivate administrators to spend time and resources on peer evaluations. In fact, the current use of student evaluations not only causes grade inflation, but it can also force faculty to teach in a defensive manner, which goes against many of the goals of a writing studies approach to composition and learning.[5] The development of a more robust system of faculty evaluation could help all aspects of research universities because it would force them to prioritize quality undergraduate education.

In the UC system, lecturers are evaluated for their teaching, service, and professional development, and while they are not expected to do research, they can receive funding to stay current with their discipline. Some critics argue that this use of nontenured faculty only increases the divide between research and teaching, but we have found that many of our contingent faculty have been productive scholars even as they focus on undergraduate instruction. As an example of reinvention from below, the unionization of these teachers has helped us place undergraduate education in a more central position because we are able to bargain directly with the administration over educational matters like class size, faculty evaluation, professional development, and instructional support.

TRANSPARENCY AND ACTIVISM

UC-AFT is also part of larger state and national organizations, so we have been able to use our pooled resources to bring issues to the state legislature and the governor. One of the main projects we have pursued with the state is to force the university to determine how much it costs to educate each undergraduate student and who is paying for this instruction. My union helped push through a state audit of the university system, and our efforts, and the work of others inside and outside the institution, have resulted in a new funding model for the university. We have also organized to get the state to audit workload at the university in order to determine how many courses are being taught by contingent faculty and the average class size of the courses.[6] These collective efforts for transparency are essential to reinventing the university, and they have been useful in producing more stable contingent faculty positions.

As we have witnessed throughout this book, it is hard to imagine implementing a writing studies pedagogy if the field continues to rely on part-time faculty hired at the last minute without experience, expertise, and degrees in teaching composition. It is also difficult to focus on what students transfer from one class and genre to the next if institutions do not increase their attention to undergraduate teaching and learning. The key then is to organize for both more stable, professional positions and more say in institutional priorities. For example, we have found that a push for more full-time positions helps increase the likelihood that faculty will be hired in an effective manner and that more instructors will be given a role in shared governance. In fact, our contract requires contingent faculty to sit on hiring and review committees.

Of course, many states do not allow for collective bargaining, but if more faculty are organized in the non-right-to-work states, the industry standard will be lifted for everyone. We are already seeing some signs that universities and colleges are increasing the wages of contingent faculty in order to prevent unionization, and the publication of salaries has helped advertise the disparities among institutions. There has also been a push to require disciplinary organizations set standards and publish wage and workload information.

THE RHETORIC OF POWER

This stress on collective action and power is needed to supplement our current reliance on the rhetoric of ethos, pathos, and logos. While many proponents of writing studies believe the field can improve its status by making a logical or ethical or emotional appeals, I have argued we need to develop a rhetoric of power to understand how social change is enacted. Moreover, this theory of power needs to think through the issues concerning collective action and social movements from the bottom up. In other words, instead of seeing institutional change as the result of people in power making better decisions, we should organize on a collective level to force people at the top to listen to people at the bottom of the social hierarchy. In the case of institutions of higher education, contingent undergraduate faculty must organize to reinvent the university and change its priorities on both a local and national level.

As Linda Adler-Kassner and Peggy O'Neill argue in *Reframing Writing Assessment*, it is also important for composition faculty and collective organizations to intervene in how policymakers talk about writing and higher education (Adler-Kassner and O'Neill 2010, 9). Part of this reframing of the public understanding of composition entails intervening in the current move to center K–12 education on testing, ranking, and grading. Since the field of writing studies has much to offer in relation to the ways people think about learning and assessment in all fields, we must play a more organized role in public policy. For instance, in previous chapters, we have seen how grading and testing limits what students learn and how they transfer knowledge from one situation to the next. Therefore, in order to continue to promote effective learning, we should join with collective organizations, like K–12 teachers' unions, to fight reductive models of assessment.

ORGANIZING WITH STUDENTS

As contingent faculty organize, they realize a key ally in their fight for workplace justice is students. Using the slogan "Faculty working conditions determine students' learning conditions," many non-tenure-track faculty have worked with student organizations to tie concerns about tuition, student debt, graduation rates, and postgraduation employment possibilities to the use and abuse of insecure faculty. Students and parents do not understand why they are paying more for higher education while the institutions appear to be putting less money into instruction. In pushing for budgetary transparency, faculty and students working together can fight to change the priorities of their institutions. A side effect of this process is that as students advocate for a more democratic institution, they begin to desire a more democratic learning environment. Here organized faculty can help show the negative effects of large classes and standardized teaching as they work with students to demand smaller classes and more interactive learning environments.

RESEARCH, THEORY, AND ACTIVISM

This stress on collective action, undergraduate education, students, and teaching may look like a dismissal of the importance of research and theory, but it should be clear that we need theory and research about university budgets in order to determine how universities are spending their money and determining their priorities. We also need a theoretical understanding of the best practices for teaching and learning, but we should realize this theory must be attached to a plan for collective action. In the case of writing studies, if we value the roles of transfer, metacognition, and genre in student learning, we need to determine how we can restructure universities to privilege these concepts. Some proponents of writing studies argue that the best way to promote these key ideas is to do research and publish more articles, but I have countered that this strategy merely repeats and reinforces the dominant research university paradigm.

Instead of trying to advance the discipline by mimicking other fields, I have been arguing that we must organize to transform our institutions from below. However, I do not think the classroom is the primary place to do this organizing. First of all, we do not want to indoctrinate our students or use grades to force them to comply with our ideologies. Also, the logic of teaching is very different from the discourse of activism. In order to clarify this point, I will differentiate teaching, researching, organizing, and writing on a conceptual level.

One of the main historical arguments of this book is derived from Robert Nisbet's (1971) argument that universities were transformed after World War II when large amounts of federal cash poured into these institutions. One of the results of this new access to funds was that separate research institutes were established, and research became separated from teaching. Furthermore, research became much more lucrative and prestigious, so teaching was increasingly relegated to nonre-searchers, and this move helped increase the number of non-tenure-track faculty and graduate-student instructors. From Nisbet's perspective, this transition meant that the pure pursuit of knowledge for knowledge's sake was replaced by the rush for money and personal advancement.

It is hard to imagine how we can completely reverse this undermining of both research and teaching by the cash nexus, but we can seek to establish protections for these different activities. The first step is to affirm that university research should be based on the ideal pursuit of objectivity, neutrality, and universality, and this ideal means personal and monetary concerns should play no role in the methodological and disciplinary search for truth. On a practical level, we should defend the need for funding pure research, but we also need to get rid of the notion that research and teaching always go hand in hand. Part of this change would mean we do not force researchers into the classroom and we stop forcing teachers to do research in order to attain job security. By rewarding effective teaching with stable positions, we can increase the quality of instruction, and by allowing some researchers to simply research, we can also protect against ineffective teaching.

One way of showing teaching and research are separate activities is by realizing that the disciplinary search for objective truth is very different from the effort to engage a diverse student body in the production and critical analysis of knowledge. Instead of being a mainly objective, neutral, and universal practice like research, teaching must adjust to particular genres and situations. As the writing studies theories of transfer and genre tell us, instruction is not a universal process but rather requires a focus on purpose, audience, context, and larger institutional and social factors. If research is a modern universal activity, teaching is inherently postmodern because it has to take into account different disciplines and student backgrounds.

In contrast to research and teaching, activism requires addressing relationships of power in a direct manner through collective action. To organize, we must recognize local contexts and universal theories, but the focus must be on framing and transforming material relationships. It is therefore important to differentiate activism from teaching and research because we do not want faculty to use their power in the classroom to manipulate students, and we also do not want to corrupt research by pursuing special interests and advocacy. Even though these may be impossible ideals, it is still important to try to respect these differences.

The way I place writing in this framework is by arguing that composition entails trying to bring together the logic of teaching, research, and activism. The difficulty of writing, then, is in part derived from the fact that it tries to integrate different activities and logics: a writer tries to research the truth and frame a perspective as they communicate with a specific audience for a specific purpose. Writing also requires the use of generalized structures and grammars as it employs knowledge of particular genres in a self-reflective manner. Furthermore, writing is a form of social activism and social construction because it seeks to intervene in how people perceive themselves and the world around them. Yet, we should not confuse activism and writing: although writing can lead to social transformation, it is often itself not a collective intervention in material relations.

This framework I am developing is highly theoretical, and thus it shows we cannot simply abandon theory, but we must realize theory is not enough, and we cannot change our institutions by simply creating better theories. Too often proponents of writing studies have sought to resolve structural problems through speculative mediations, and these theoretical responses have often replicated the worst aspects of the dominant research-university paradigm. Instead of advocating conformity to the current system, I have called for a disruptive model of teaching, writing, and activism.

In terms of teaching, this emphasis on dissensus, complexity, difference, and disruption means we have to challenge the current stress on grading, assessing, ranking, and rating. As Adler-Kassner and O'Neill (2010, 45–46) reveal, the history of composition has been tied to a logic of assessment that itself has much to do with a reductive understanding of learning. As a form of management science, measuring and controlling student error and success has resulted in framing composition as a system of social control.[7] Adler-Kassner and O'Neill also point out that the high workload for reading and grading student papers has motivated institutions to call for a model of efficiency requiring the use of part-time faculty and graduate students who are instructed to focus on form and not content. Conceptions of writing, assessment, and academic labor are thus interconnected, and it is therefore necessary to determine how collective action can reframe these issues.

THE CULTURE OF CYNICAL CONFORMITY

I have argued that a major reason it is so hard to change our institutions is that all levels of education are now dominated by a culture of cynical conformity in which institutions, teachers, and students try to outcompete each other in a system in which no one really believes. For example, at the same time universities criticize ranking systems like *US News & World Report*'s, they spend resources to move up in the rankings. Likewise, faculty and administrators know large classes are often ineffective, but they use them anyway because they see no alternative. Moreover, departments judge contingent faculty by student evaluations as they critique these superficial indicators of teaching quality, and students try to outdo each other for grades, even though they do not feel engaged in their learning. We thus live in a culture of cynical conformity, and any real educational change must work against this type of socialization.

We know that as societies become more unequal, social trust is reduced, and a vicious cycle of cynical conformity is initiated in which people do not want to support public programs because they do not believe in their inherent value.[8] In terms of higher education, the more unequal our society becomes, the less people are willing to pay taxes to help other people succeed. Likewise, the more school officials and politicians argue that a college degree leads to earning more money, the more a public good is transformed into a private good, and once people think of college as a private good, they see no reason to support it with their taxes. After all, why should a parent help pay for the education of another student who is competing with their child for a small number of good jobs?

In order to reframe this issue, we should stop selling higher education as the pathway to good jobs and more money. Not only does the current strategy undermine public funding for public institutions, but it changes the way students approach their own education. Since students have been told college is now only about future employment, they have less interest in pursuing knowledge for knowledge's sake.[9] Moreover, since school is being tied to the competition for a decreasing number of good jobs, students are not encouraged to cooperate with each other and learn from their peers. Also, as we have seen, the focus on degrees and jobs enhances the focus on grades, which often blocks the ability of students to learn and transfer new knowledge. As educators and teachers of writing, we must take on these larger social trends in a direct way through collective action.

Not only should we research how the emphasis on jobs and grades affects student learning, but we must also work with larger organizations to promote a different vision of what education should entail. As teachers, we should be aware of how this framing of learning affects students in the classroom as we push our own institutions to promote a more expansive notion of learning. If instead of framing higher education as career preparation and individual prosperity we stress the role college plays in improving society and making life more just and rewarding for everyone, we can return to the idea of higher education as a public good. Part of this effort requires promoting a vision of educational and democratic citizenship. If we use our classrooms as models for social engagement, we can help define and enhance the ways our students think about their roles in the larger society.

NOTES

1. See Maitland and Rhoades (2005).
2. It is estimated that, not including graduate students, 60–80 percent of all people teaching college composition are off the tenure track (see Hassel 2013).
3. In 2012, the average annual salary for the over three thousand UC non-tenure-track faculty was $62,000, with an average full course load of six courses on semester campuses. These numbers mean the per-course pay was over $10,000, while the national average appears to be around $3,000. Moreover, unlike most other faculty working outside the tenure system, UC lecturers who work more than half time have full medical, dental, and vision care, and they participate in a defined benefits pension plan. This model of labor justice is protected by a detailed contract, which defends many of the faculty against job insecurity. Similar to the traditional tenure-track career path, non-tenure-track faculty in the UC system go up for a comprehensive review in their sixth year of teaching, and if they are deemed excellent, they are given a continuing appointment, which means they can only be let go for just cause or a proven lack of instructional need. A key aspect to the contract regulating these faculty members is that it recognizes the diverse employment needs of contingent faculty members. Except for benefits, all rights and salary policies apply to all faculty members regardless of whether they teach a single course or a full load. By basing compensation on a percentage appointment, the university is able to cater to its particular needs, while the union is able to provide for a just and fair wage and work level. While a third of these teachers work full time, another third teach only one or two courses a year.
4. While it is difficult to organize in right-to-work states, it is not impossible, Moreover, when unions bring up the standards for workers in one area, it tends to have an effect on all related workers.
5. See Samuels (2013, 111, 125).
6. In the UC system, lecturers are often given course credit and pay for extensive departmental or university service. For example, many of the UC writing programs are staffed by full-time lecturers who teach most of the courses and do most of the administration. While the full-time maximum course load is nine courses for the campuses on the quarter system, a course load of eight courses is considered a 100 percent appointment for teachers of writing and languages. The contract also provides a method for faculty to petition for course credit for nonrequired duties, such as proctoring exams and external outreach.
7. Adler-Kassner and O'Neill (2010, 45–46).
8. For more on the relation between social trust and inequality, see Wilkinson and Pickett (2011).
9. See Samuels (2013, 31–32).

REFERENCES

Adler-Kassner, Linda, and Peggy O'Neill. 2010. *Reframing Writing Assessment to Improve Teaching and Learning.* Logan: Utah State University Press.

Adler-Kassner, Linda, and Elizabeth Wardle. 2015. *Naming What We Know: Threshold Concepts of Writing Studies.* Logan: Utah State University Press.

Althusser, Louis. 2006. "Ideology and Ideological State Apparatuses (Notes Towards an Investigation)." In *The Anthropology of the State: A Reader*, 86–111. Hoboken, NJ: John Wiley & Sons.

Bartholomae, David. 1985. *Inventing the University.* New York: Guilford.

Baudrillard, Jean. 1993. *The Transparency of Evil: Essays on Extreme Phenomena.* London: Verso.

Bazerman, Charles. 2012. "Genre as Social Action." In *The Routledge Handbook of Discourse Analysis*, edited by James Paul Gee and Michael Handford, 226–38. New York: Routledge.

Beaufort, Anne. 2007. *College Writing and Beyond: A New Framework for University Writing Instruction.* Logan: Utah State University Press.

Becher, Tony, and Paul Trowler. 2001. *Academic Tribes and Territories: Intellectual Enquiry and the Culture of Disciplines.* London: McGraw-Hill Education.

Bereiter, Carl. 1995. "A Dispositional View of Transfer." In *Teaching for Transfer: Fostering Generalization in Learning*, edited by Anne McKeough, Judy Lupart, and Anthony Marini, 21–34. Mahwah, NJ: Lawrence Erlbaum.

Bloom, Paul. 2014. "Against Empathy." *Boston Review*, September 10.

Bosley, Lisa. 2008. "'I Don't Teach Reading': Critical Reading Instruction in Composition Courses." *Literacy Research and Instruction* 47 (4): 285–308. http://dx.doi.org/10.1080/19388070802332861.

Bousquet, Marc. 2008. *How the University Works.* New York: New York University Press.

Bousquet, Marc, Tony Scott, and Leo Parascondola, eds. 2004. *Tenured Bosses and Disposable Teachers: Writing Instruction in the Managed University.* Carbondale: Southern Illinois University Press.

Costa, Arthur L., and Bena Kallick. 2009. *Habits of Mind Across the Curriculum: Practical and Creative Strategies for Teachers.* Alexandria, VA: Association for Supervision and Curriculum Development.

Crowley, Sharon. 1998. *Composition in the University: Historical and Polemical Essays.* Pittsburgh, PA: University of Pittsburgh Press.

Damasio, Antonio. 2008. *Descartes' Error: Emotion, Reason, and the Human Brain.* New York: Random House.

Derrida, Jacques. 1978. *Writing and Difference.* Chicago, IL: University of Chicago Press.

DOI: 10.7330/9781607325840.c007

Descartes, René. 1996. *Discourse on the Method: And, Meditations on First Philosophy.* New Haven: Yale University Press. http://dx.doi.org/10.1017/CBO9780511 805028.

Dobrin, Sidney I. 2011. *Postcomposition.* Carbondale: Southern Illinois University Press.

Douglas, Susan J. 2010. *The Rise of Enlightened Sexism: How Pop Culture Took Us from Girl Power to Girls Gone Wild.* New York: Macmillan.

Downs, Douglas, and Elizabeth Wardle. 2007. "Teaching about Writing, Righting Misconceptions:(Re) Envisioning 'First-Year Composition' as 'Introduction to Writing Studies.'" *College Composition and Communication* 58 (4): 552–84.

Eagan, M. Kevin, and Audrey J. Jaeger. 2008. "Closing the Gate: Part Time Faculty Instruction in Gatekeeper Courses and First Year Persistence." *New Directions for Teaching and Learning* 2008 (115): 39–53. http://dx.doi.org/10.1002 /tl.324.

Easterly, William. 2014. *The Tyranny of Experts.* New York: Basic Civitas Books.

Fisher, Mark. 2009. *Capitalist Realism: Is There No Alternative?* London: John Hunt.

Foster, Hal. 1985. *Recodings: Art, Spectacle, Cultural Politics.* Hayward, CA: Bay.

Hassel, Holly. 2013. "Research Gaps in Teaching English in the Two-Year College." *Teaching English in the Two Year College* 40 (4): 343.

Hayek, Friedrich August. 1945. "The Use of Knowledge in Society." *American Economic Review* 35 (4): 519–30.

Hayes, Christopher. 2013. *Twilight of the Elites: America after Meritocracy.* New York: Broadway Books.

Hickok, Gregory. 2014. *The Myth of Mirror Neurons: The Real Neuroscience of Communication and Cognition.* New York: W.W. Norton.

Horowitz, David. 2012. *The Professors: The 101 Most Dangerous Academics in America.* Washington, DC: Regnery.

Hutcheon, Linda. 1988. "Historiographic Metafiction." In *Hutcheon, The Canadian Postmodern: A Study of Contemporary English-Canadian Fiction,* ed. Linda Hutcheon, 61–77. Oxford: Oxford University Press.

Jessop, Bob. 1993. "Towards a Schumpeterian Workfare State? Preliminary Remarks on Post-Fordist Political Economy." *Studies in Political Economy* 40: 7–39.

Kahneman, Daniel. 2011. *Thinking, Fast and Slow.* New York: Macmillan.

Karatani, Kojin. 2014. *The Structure of World History: From Modes of Production to Modes of Exchange.* Durham, NC: Duke University Press. http://dx.doi.org /10.1215/9780822376682.

Kellner, Douglas. 2002. "New Media and New Literacies: Reconstructing Education for the New Millennium." In *The Handbook of New Media,* edited by Leah Lievrouw and Sonia Livingstone, 90–104. New York: Sage.

Kelly, Colm. 2012. "Derrida in the University, or the Liberal Arts in Deconstruction." *Canadian Journal of Higher Education* 42 (2): 49–66.

Kirp, David L. 2009. *Shakespeare, Einstein, and the Bottom Line: The Marketing of Higher Education.* Cambridge, MA: Harvard University Press.

Klein, Naomi. 1999. *No Logo: Taking on the Brand Bullies.* New York: Picador.

Kohn, Alfie. 2000. *The Case Against Standardized Testing: Raising the Scores, Ruining the schools.* Portsmouth, NH: Heinemann.

Labaree, David F. 2012. *Someone Has to Fail.* Cambridge, MA: Harvard University Press.

Lacan, Jacques. 1998. *The Four Fundamental Concepts of Psycho-Analysis.* New York: W.W. Norton.

Lasch, Christopher. 1998. *The Culture of Narcissism: American Life in an Age of Diminishing Expectations.* New York: W.W. Norton.

Lauer, Janice M. 1984. "Composition Studies: Dappled Discipline." *Rhetoric Review* 3 (1): 20–29. http://dx.doi.org/10.1080/07350198409359074.

Magill, R. Jay. 2009. *Chic Ironic Bitterness.* Ann Arbor: University of Michigan Press.

Maitland, Christine, and Gary Rhoades. 2005. "Bargaining for Contingent Faculty." In *The NEA 2005 Almanac of Higher Education.*

Marx, Karl. 1975. "Contribution to the Critique of Hegel's Philosophy of Law." In *Collected Works* 3: 3–129. London: Lawrence and Wishart.

Miller, Carolyn R. 1984. "Genre as Social Action." *Quarterly Journal of Speech* 70 (2): 151–67. http://dx.doi.org/10.1080/00335638409383686.

Mohan, Bernard A., and Winnie Au Yeung Lo. 1985. "Academic Writing and Chinese Students: Transfer and Developmental Factors." *TESOL Quarterly* 19 (3): 515–34. http://dx.doi.org/10.2307/3586276.

Newfield, Christopher. 2008. *Unmaking the Public University: The Forty-Year Assault on the Middle Class.* Cambridge, MA: Harvard University Press.

Nisbet, Robert A. 1971. *The Degradation of the Academic Dogma.* New York: Transaction.

Pariser, Eli. 2011. *The Filter Bubble: What the Internet Is Hiding from You.* London: Penguin Books.

Perkins, David N., and Gavriel Salomon. 1992. "Transfer of Learning." International Encyclopedia of Education 2. Oxford: Pergamon Press.

Pope, Denise Clark. 2001. *Doing School: How We Are Creating a Generation of Stressed Out, Materialistic, and Miseducated Students.* New Haven: Yale University Press.

Powell, John A. 2008. "Post-Racialism or Targeted Universalism." *Denver University Law Review* 86:785.

Ravitch, Diane. 2013. *Reign of Error: The Hoax of the Privatization Movement and the Danger to America's Public Schools.* New York: Vintage.

Readings, Bill. 1996. *The University in Ruins.* Cambridge, MA: Harvard University Press.

Riniolo, Todd C., Katherine C. Johnson, Tracy R. Sherman, and Julie A. Misso. 2006. "Hot or Not: Do Professors Perceived as Physically Attractive Receive Higher Student Evaluations?" *Journal of General Psychology* 133 (1): 19–35. http://dx.doi.org/10.3200/GENP.133.1.19-35.

Robertson, Linda, and James Slevin. 1987. "The Status of Composition Faculty: Resolving Reforms." *Rhetoric Review* 5 (2): 190–93. http://dx.doi.org/10.1080/07350198709359144.

Lewontin, R. C., Steven Rose, and Leon J. Kamin. 1984. *Not in Our Genes: Biology, Ideology, and Human Nature.* New York: Pantheon.

Samuels, Robert. 2013. *Why Public Higher Education Should Be Free.* New Brunswick, NJ: Rutgers University Press.

Schell, Eileen, and Patricia L. Stock, eds. 2000. *Moving a Mountain: Transforming the Role of Contingent Faculty in Composition Studies and Higher Education.* Urbana, IL: NCTE.

Scott, Tony. 2009. *Dangerous Writing: Understanding the Political Economy of Composition.* Logan: Utah State University Press.

Skidmore, David. 2000. "From Pedagogical Dialogue to Dialogical Pedagogy." *Language and Education* 14 (4): 283–96. http://dx.doi.org/10.1080/095007 80008666794.

Sledd, James. 2001. "On Buying In and Selling Out: A Note for Bosses Old and New." *College Composition and Communication* 53 (1): 146–49. http://dx.doi.org /10.2307/359066.

Sloterdijk, Peter. 1988. *Critique of Cynical Reason.* Minneapolis: University of Minnesota Press.

Smit, David W. 2004. *The End of Composition Studies.* Carbondale: Southern Illinois University Press.

Stark, Philip B., and Richard Freishtat. 2014. *An Evaluation of Course Evaluations.* Berkley: University of California Center for Teaching and Learning. http://senate.csusb.edu/Reports/evaluations_paper.pdf.

Strickland, Donna. 2011. *The Managerial Unconscious in the History of Composition Studies.* Carbondale: Southern Illinois University Press.

Strinati, Dominic. 1993. "The Big Nothing? Contemporary Culture and the Emergence of Postmodernism." *Innovation* 6 (3): 359–74. http://dx.doi.org /10.1080/13511610.1993.9968362.

Taber, Michael W. 2010. "I Know I Shouldn't Generalize, But—: A Rhetorical Critique of Ethnography in Composition Studies." PhD dissertation, University of South Florida, Tampa.

Tannock, Stuart. 2008. "The Problem of Education Based Discrimination." *British Journal of Sociology of Education* 29 (5): 439–49. http://dx.doi.org/10.1080 /01425690802326846.

Tewdwr-Jones, Mark, and Philip Allmendinger. 1998. "Deconstructing Communicative Rationality: A Critique of Habermasian Collaborative Planning." *Environment & Planning* 30 (11): 1975–89. http://dx.doi.org/10.1068/a301 975.

Trout, Paul. 1998. "Deconstructing an Evaluation form." *Montana Professor* 8 (3). http://mtprof.msun.edu/Fall1998/TroutArt.html.

Turner, Fred. 2010. *From Counterculture to Cyberculture: Stewart Brand, the Whole Earth Network, and the Rise of Digital Utopianism.* Chicago: University of Chicago Press.

Villanueva, Victor. 2001. "The Politics of Literacy Across the Curriculum." In *WAC for the New Millennium: Strategies for Continuing Writing-Across-the-Curriculum Programs,* edited by Susan H. McLeod, 165–78. Urbana: National Council of Teachers of English.

Walvoord, Barbara E. 1996. "The Future of WAC." *College English* 58 (1): 58–79. http://dx.doi.org/10.2307/378534.

Wardle, Elizabeth. 2013. "Intractable Writing Program Problems, 'Kairos,' and Writing about Writing: A Profile of the University of Central Florida's First-Year Composition Program." *Composition Forum* 27.

Washburn, Jennifer. 2008. *University, Inc.: The Corporate Corruption of Higher Education.* New York: Basic Books.

Wilkinson, Richard, and Kate Pickett. 2011. *The Spirit Level: Why Greater Equality Makes Societies Stronger.* New York: Bloomsbury.

Yancey, Kathleen Blake, Liane Robertson, and Kara Taczak. 2014. *Writing across Contexts: Transfer, Composition, and Sites of Writing.* Logan: Utah State University Press.

Young, Michael Dunlop. 1958. *The Rise of the Meritocracy.* Piscataway, NJ: Transaction.

Žižek, Slavoy. 1989. *The Sublime Object of Ideology.* London: Verso.

ABOUT THE AUTHOR

ROBERT SAMUELS teaches writing at the University of California, Santa Barbara and is the author of eight books, including the influential *Why Public Higher Education Should Be Free: How to Reduce Costs and Improve Instruction at American Universities*. He is president of the faculty union UC-AFT. He writes the blog *Changing Universities*.

INDEX